Getting to Know Jesus

Mark

Kevin Perrotta
Gerald Darring

**Six Weeks
with the Bible
for Catholic Teens**

6

Exploring
God's Word

LOYOLAPRESS.
CHICAGO

LOYOLAPRESS.

3441 N. ASHLAND AVENUE
CHICAGO, ILLINOIS 60657
(800) 621-1008
WWW.LOYOLABOOKS.ORG

Nihil Obstat
Reverend John G. Lodge, S.S.L., S.T.D.
Censor Deputatus
May 30, 2004

Imprimatur
Most Reverend Edwin M. Conway, D.D.
Vicar General
Archdiocese of Chicago
June 7, 2004

The *Nihil Obstat* and *Imprimatur* are official declarations that a book is free of doctrinal and moral error. No implication is contained therein that those who have granted the *Nihil Obstat* and *Imprimatur* agree with the content, opinions, or statements expressed.

Scripture excerpts are from the New Revised Standard Version Bible, © 1989, Division of Christian Education of the National Council of the Churches of Christ in the United States of America. Used by permission. All rights reserved. Subheadings in Scripture quotations have been added by Kevin Perrotta.

Excerpts from Vatican conciliar, postconciliar, and papal documents are from the official translations, Libreria Editrice Vaticana, 00120 Citta del Vaticano.

60–61 The Latin text (with an English translation) of Thomas More, *Concerning the Sorrow, Weariness, Fear, and Prayer of Christ before His Arrest* can be found in Clarence H. Miller, trans., *The Complete Works of St. Thomas More*, vol. 14, pt. 1 (New Haven, Conn.: Yale University Press, 1976). Translation by the author.

Cover and Interior Design: Th!nk Design Group

ISBN 0-8294-2082-7

Printed in the United States of America.
       07 08 Bang 5 4 3

Contents

How to Use This Guide

You might compare this volume to a short visit to a national park. The park is so large that you could spend months, even years, getting to know it. But a brief visit, if carefully planned, can be worthwhile. In a few hours you can drive through the park and pull over at a handful of sites. At each stop you can get out of the car, take a short trail through the woods, listen to the wind blowing in the trees, and get a feel for the place.

In this volume we'll travel through the Gospel of Mark, making half a dozen stops along the way. At those points we'll proceed on foot, taking a leisurely walk through the selected passages. The readings have been chosen to take us to the heart of Mark's message about Jesus. After each discussion we'll get back in the car and take the highway to the next stop. "Between Discussions" pages summarize the portions of Mark that we will pass along the way.

This guide provides everything you need either to explore the Gospel of Mark in six discussions or to do a six-part exploration on your own. The introduction on page 6 will prepare you to get the most out of your reading. The weekly sections feature key passages from Mark, with explanations that highlight what his words mean for us today. Equally important, each section supplies questions that will launch you into fruitful discussion, helping you both to explore Mark for yourself and to learn from one another. If you're using the volume by yourself, the questions will spur your personal reflection.

Each discussion is meant to be a *guided discovery*.

Guided ~ None of us is equipped to read the Bible without help. We read the Bible *for* ourselves but not *by* ourselves. Scripture was written to be understood and applied in and with the Church. So each week "A Guide to the Reading," drawing on the work of both modern biblical scholars and Christian writers of the past, supplies background and explanations. The guide will help you grasp Mark's message. Think of it as a friendly park ranger who points out noteworthy details and explains what you're looking at so you can appreciate things for yourself.

Discovery ~ The purpose is for *you* to interact with Mark's Gospel. "Questions for a Closer Look" is a tool to help you dig into the Gospel and examine it carefully. "Questions for Application" will help you discern what Mark means for your life here and now. Each week concludes with an "Approach to Prayer" section that helps you respond to God's Word. Supplementary "Living Tradition" and "Saints in the Making" sections offer the thoughts and experiences of Christians past and present in order to show you what the Gospel has meant to others—so that you can consider what it might mean for you.

If you are using this volume for individual study, pay special attention to the questions provided for each week (Warm-Up Questions, Questions for a Closer Look, Questions for Application). One advantage of individual study is that you can take all the time you need to consider all the questions. You may also want to read the Gospel of Mark in its entirety, and you will find that the "Between Discussions" pages will help you understand the additional portions of the Gospel. Finally, take your time making your way through the Gospel of Mark and this accompanying volume: let your reading be an opportunity for this Gospel to become God's words to you.

Unexpected Good News

Introducing Mark's Gospel

Our *Town,* Thornton Wilder's play about life in a New England village, opened on Broadway in 1938. Today, more than 60 years later, many high school students still see or read the play as part of their English curriculum.

The play opens with the Stage Manager walking onto an empty stage to set the scene. "The name of the town," he tells the audience, "is Grover's Corners, New Hampshire—just across the Massachusetts line: latitude 42°40'; longitude 70°37'. The first act shows a day in our town. The day is May 7, 1901. The time is just before dawn."

Later the Stage Manager brings a local professor on stage to tell the audience about the geology of the region and the American Indians who had lived there in centuries past.

By providing the audience with the real space-time coordinates and the historical background of the town, the playwright suggests that the lives of its residents have universal meaning.

When Mark wrote his Gospel, he did not put an informative stage manager at the beginning of his work. He dives right into the story. It might have helped us appreciate the importance of his story if he had written an introduction, however. Indeed, when Matthew and Luke sat down to adapt Mark and write their own Gospels, they each added a couple of introductory chapters.

An *Our Town*-style introduction to the Gospel of Mark might include a guide standing on a hillside, looking down at a cluster of stone houses in the valley. "The name of this town," he says, "is Nazareth in Galilee. Galilee is a hilly region rising up from the Mediterranean to the west and descending eastward to the lake we call the Sea of Galilee. The lake's been there for five million years, since the earth split open and formed the Great Rift that stretches from Lebanon to Africa.

"This area's seen a lot of comings and goings. Some 30 thousand years ago, Neanderthal people kept house in a cave yonder. It's almost two thousand years since Abraham traveled through these hills. Israelites settled here a thousand years ago. According to your modern reckoning, the year is A.D. 30."

Such an introduction might have prepared us to appreciate the contrast between his story's small scale and its importance for the whole world. Mark's Gospel covers events that seemed insignificant to most people at the time. Mark tells about the brief life and untimely death of a man from an obscure village—a man hardly mentioned by anyone at the time besides his own followers. Yet before there were any Israelites, before prehistoric people lived in caves, before the shaping of the earth, this man, Jesus of Nazareth, had been at the center of God's plan for humanity.

The play *Our Town* speaks to all of us because it helps us understand what it means to be a human being. Mark's Gospel speaks to all of us because it tells about what God has done to change the human condition.

Pattern, promises, and expectations ~ Mark may not have given his Gospel an introduction because he thought it already had one: the Scriptures of Israel. He points out in his first verses that the gospel, or "Good News," of Jesus unfolded in line with what God promised through the prophets of Israel.

Mark saw Jesus as the climax of what God had been doing with Israel. This means that it is important for us to know about God's dealings with Israel if we are to understand who Jesus was and what he came to do. Let's look briefly at the background.

The Scriptures of Israel, which Christians call the Old Testament, portray a single creator, who has made us in his likeness, designed to be in a relationship with him (Genesis 1:26). The God of the Old Testament is just, yet forgiving; he is a God both majestic and merciful (Sirach 2:18). The Old Testament portrays us as noble creatures who tend to set ourselves in conflict with God—and with each other.

The Old Testament shows that God focused his love for the human race on a small Near-Eastern people called Israel. God rescued the Israelites from their enemies. He formed a covenant—a permanent, faithful bond—with them. He instructed them in how to worship and trust him and in how to live in faithfulness and peace with one another. The Israelites did not always respond wholeheartedly to God, and they would suffer the painful consequences of their sins. When they turned back to God, he would renew his relationship with them and help them in their need.

In 587 B.C. the people of Israel, guilty of idolatries and social injustices, witnessed the destruction of Jerusalem by the Babylonians. This disaster was a turning point in their history. God promised the Jews a splendid restoration. He would forgive their sins and even heal their sinful hearts (Jeremiah 31:31–34). Exiles would return to the land of Israel (Zephaniah 3:14–20). The Jerusalem Temple would be rebuilt, and God would dwell there gloriously at the center of his people (Ezekiel 40—48). There would be prosperity for the people of Israel and defeat for their enemies (Zechariah 14). But God's blessings on the Jews would benefit the rest of the human race as well (Zechariah 8:20–23).

Six centuries later, at the beginning of the first century, these promises seemed to have been only half fulfilled. The land of Israel was part of the Roman Empire—a situation that pious Jews found difficult to accept. In spite of their situation, however, the Jews' expectations for God's intervention intensified. Many of them expected God to take decisive action and bring human history to an end. God, they thought, would come to reign as king in a final age of justice and peace. Even the dead would rise to enjoy new life. These high expectations, combined with their political and economic suffering, led the Jews to rise up against the Romans on many occasions. Eventually two unsuccessful rebellions against Rome, in A.D. 66–70 and 132–135, resulted in catastrophe for the Jews.

In this tense situation, around A.D. 30, Jesus made an electrifying declaration: the period of waiting is over! God's reign is about to arrive! (1:14–15). Jesus claimed to be the fulfillment of God's dealings with Israel and the fully authorized representative of Israel's God. Everything that Jesus said and did should have made it clear to the Jews of his time that their expectations for God's action on their behalf were being fulfilled.

Expected, yet surprising ~ But it quickly became apparent that Jesus was fulfilling Jewish expectations in a very unexpected way. Jews of the time who observed Jesus and listened to his preaching would have found several aspects of his "program" surprising.

A messiah greater than expected ~ Jews had various expectations of how God would act on their behalf. Some thought God would appoint a special person, a messiah, to take the lead in doing God's work. But Jews hardly expected a messiah to act with the divine authority that Jesus claimed to have. The Kingdom of God was becoming present in *Jesus'* words and touch. The restoration of Israel began as men and women took their places in the company of *Jesus'* disciples (see 3:33–35). Equally remarkable, Jesus gave authoritative rulings on Israel's basic, God-given law (2:23–28). As God's representative, he forgave sins (2:1–11).

A more radical program ~ The prophets had predicted military triumph and national sovereignty, but Jesus did not aim at a literal fulfillment of those predictions. He did not raise an army to liberate the land of Israel, but instead promoted a kingdom without ties to any particular land. Jesus did bring liberation, but not from the Romans. He liberated people from sicknesses, guilt, sinful attitudes, and broken relationships.

Jesus also did not say that God would increase his presence in the Temple in Jerusalem. In fact, he performed an action in the Temple symbolizing that the Temple would not be needed anymore (11:15–17).

Jesus bypassed the Mosaic rule permitting divorce. Instead, he challenged people to maintain marital permanence through a change of heart (10:2–12).

Thus Jesus reinterpreted Israel's central values: Promised Land, Jerusalem Temple, and Mosaic law. He was aiming at a deeper liberation and restoration than expected. He wanted a renewal of people's hearts, so that they might become what God created them to be.

Jesus did not undertake a mission to non-Jews, but he opened the way for them to share in God's Kingdom by shifting the focus of God's activity from what was essential to the Jews: land, temple, and law. On occasion he used his miraculous powers to aid non-Jews as well as Jews (7:24—8:10).

A kingdom now but not yet ~ Jews in the first century had different opinions on the subject of the last days. Most of them did not expect the world to end. They thought God would change the world and begin a new, final age of holiness and peace. When Jesus declared that God's Kingdom was about to arrive, he was indicating that this final age was beginning. Yet it was not coming down from heaven with power and glory. It was springing up in small, seemingly insignificant ways (chapter 4). The final age of God's loving care for men and women was beginning. It would bring forgiveness and healing and God's guiding Spirit, but it would not bring an immediate end to suffering and persecution (8:34–38; 10:29–30). Unexpectedly, God's reign was both present and still to come.

A suffering messiah ~ Most surprising was the way Jesus understood the chief task God had given him. Jesus shocked his followers by informing them that, in fulfillment of God's purposes, he was going to allow himself to be arrested, tortured, and executed by the religious and political authorities; after this, he would rise from the dead (8:31). The Jews expected resurrection in the final age, but not the humiliating death of the Messiah.

How we can connect with the story ~ If Jesus had been what the Jews of the time expected, his life might not have had much meaning for us, since we are not Jews living in the land of Israel in the early first century. We find meaning in Jesus' life because of the unexpected way he fulfilled God's promises. Our reading of Mark's Gospel will show us how Jesus' surprising fulfillment of God's promises to Israel is very good news for us. Before we begin, we should review a couple of themes in Mark that may help God's message to come through in reading the Gospel.

The secret of Jesus' identity ~ People reacted to Jesus with both admiration and fear, faith and consternation. They found it hard to ignore him because he spoke and acted with authority, he supported his claims with miracles, and he attracted large crowds. They had to wrestle with the question of who he was (1:27; 6:2–3). Was he a nobody, nothing more than a carpenter from Nazareth, who was leading people astray from God's covenant with Israel? Or was he someone much greater than that? Even the men and women who became his disciples struggled to understand him. Sometimes they were baffled and terrified trying to follow a man who rejected earthly ambitions and seemed to welcome crucifixion (10:32–34).

Jesus exercised his authority openly, Mark says, but he was quiet about who he was. He would sometimes tell the people he had healed not to tell others about their healing (1:43–44; 5:43). The demons knew who he was, and he ordered them to be silent (1:34). He told his disciples not to tell others what they knew about him (8:30; 9:9). He referred to himself as "the Son of Man" (2:10,28; 8:31), a term that would intrigue his listeners but did little to help them understand who he was.

Mark's Gospel uses several titles for Jesus—Messiah, King, Son of David. The title that best expresses Jesus' identity and his relationship with God is Son of God (1:11). This is how God thinks of Jesus. Jesus kept this title secret until his trial (14:61–62). Mark's Gospel is thus the drama of Jesus being revealed and recognized as the Son of God. The dramatic interest lies in whether the people around Jesus will come to grasp who he is.

Mark does not keep his readers guessing about who Jesus is. He tells us plainly at the outset that Jesus is God's Son (1:1). He lets us hear God's declaration at Jesus' baptism that Jesus is his divine son (1:11)—a declaration not heard by the human bystanders. We watch the people around Jesus struggling to discover who he is, but we already know.

Or at least we think we do. The people in the story struggle to figure out who Jesus really is, while we are tempted to pat ourselves on our backs for knowing it already. But do we really know Jesus any better than the people in the Gospel? Mark invites us to enter into the drama of his Gospel by asking ourselves questions about how well *we* recognize Jesus. What, after all, does it mean to *know* Jesus, the Son of God? Do we know Jesus if all we know is that his title is the Son of God? How well do we know Jesus? What does knowing Jesus mean for our lives? If we keep these questions in mind, our reading of Mark's Gospel will give us a chance to learn more about Jesus, to increase our experience of him and our commitment to him.

The disciples' mediocre response ~ After Jesus began to preach, his first act was to call a handful of men to become his disciples (1:16–20). From then until the moment of his arrest, he was constantly surrounded by his followers, who included women as well as men (15:40–41). Jesus kept his disciples close to him, teaching them and letting them share in his work (3:14; 4:10–11; 6:7–13).

At times, Jesus' disciples would show signs of understanding what he was about (8:29). They took steps toward genuine discipleship (1:16–20; 10:28). But they did not always set good examples of how to follow Jesus. Sometimes they seemed not to want to know the truth about Jesus (8:14–21). They even tried to stand in his way as he sought to carry out God's plans (8:32). When he was arrested, they embarrassed him by running away and even denying any relationship with him (14:50,66–71).

Mark portrays Jesus of Nazareth as someone for whom people were willing to leave everything. They were excited by his promise to bring Israel's hopes to fulfillment. Yet it was not easy for them to follow him because the way he talked about fulfilling God's plans was so unexpected. When they tried to follow him, their weaknesses were revealed. Their "first round" of discipleship—the round we see in Mark's Gospel—ended in failure.

Mark invites us to enter into the story. He invites us to see ourselves in the disciples, responding enthusiastically to Jesus and his mission. That is how we would like to be! But when the disciples fail to understand Jesus, when they try to get in his way, when they abandon him, we have second thoughts. We have to ask ourselves if we share these same tendencies. These tendencies led the first disciples to abandon Jesus; what might the same tendencies lead us to do? If we see something of ourselves in the first disciples and do not like it, what are we going to do about it?

These are serious questions. But then, Mark relates a serious story. We are only ready to read Mark's Gospel if we are serious about facing the deepest questions about God and ourselves. Only then will we be able to understand its unexpected Good News.

Are you serious?

The Kingdom of God Has Come Near

Warm-Up Questions

1 What do you like to eat at home? at school? when you're out with friends?

2 What are you like in the morning?
- ○ I like getting up early, but not too early.
- ○ I'd just as well sleep away the whole morning.
- ○ I like lying in bed, half awake and half asleep.
- ○ Please don't talk to me before 10:00 A.M.

Opening the Bible

Mark 1:1–39

The Advance Man

1:1 The beginning of the good news of Jesus Christ, the Son of God. 2 As it is written in the prophet Isaiah,

> "See, I am sending my messenger ahead of you,
> who will prepare your way;
> 3 the voice of one crying out in the wilderness:
> 'Prepare the way of the Lord,
> make his paths straight,'"

4 John the baptizer appeared in the wilderness, proclaiming a baptism of repentance for the forgiveness of sins. 5 And people from the whole Judean countryside and all the people of Jerusalem were going out to him, and were baptized by him in the river Jordan, confessing their sins. 6 Now John was clothed with camel's hair, with a leather belt around his waist, and he ate locusts and wild honey. 7 He proclaimed, "The one who is more powerful than I is coming after me; I am not worthy to stoop down and untie the thong of his sandals. 8 I have baptized you with water; but he will baptize you with the Holy Spirit."

9 In those days Jesus came from Nazareth of Galilee and was baptized by John in the Jordan. 10 And just as he was coming up out of the water, he saw the heavens torn apart and the Spirit descending like a dove on him. 11 And a voice came from heaven, "You are my Son, the Beloved; with you I am well pleased."

12 And the Spirit immediately drove him out into the wilderness. 13 He was in the wilderness forty days, tempted by Satan; and he was with the wild beasts; and the angels waited on him.

14 Now after John was arrested, Jesus came to Galilee, proclaiming the good news of God, 15 and saying, "The time is fulfilled, and the kingdom of God has come near; repent, and believe in the good news."

A Day in the Life

16 As Jesus passed along the Sea of Galilee, he saw Simon and his brother Andrew casting a net into the sea—for they were

fishermen. ¹⁷ And Jesus said to them, "Follow me and I will make you fish for people." ¹⁸ And immediately they left their nets and followed him. ¹⁹ As he went a little farther, he saw James son of Zebedee and his brother John, who were in their boat mending the nets. ²⁰ Immediately he called them; and they left their father Zebedee in the boat with the hired men, and followed him.

²¹ They went to Capernaum; and when the sabbath came, he entered the synagogue and taught. ²² They were astounded at his teaching, for he taught them as one having authority, and not as the scribes. ²³ Just then there was in their synagogue a man with an unclean spirit, ²⁴ and he cried out, "What have you to do with us, Jesus of Nazareth? Have you come to destroy us? I know who you are, the Holy One of God." ²⁵ But Jesus rebuked him, saying, "Be silent, and come out of him!" ²⁶ And the unclean spirit, convulsing him and crying with a loud voice, came out of him. ²⁷ They were all amazed, and they kept on asking one another, "What is this? A new teaching—with authority! He commands even the unclean spirits, and they obey him." ²⁸ At once his fame began to spread throughout the surrounding region of Galilee.

²⁹ As soon as they left the synagogue, they entered the house of Simon and Andrew, with James and John. ³⁰ Now Simon's mother-in-law was in bed with a fever, and they told him about her at once. ³¹ He came and took her by the hand and lifted her up. Then the fever left her, and she began to serve them.

³² That evening, at sundown, they brought to him all who were sick or possessed with demons. ³³ And the whole city was gathered around the door. ³⁴ And he cured many who were sick with various diseases, and cast out many demons; and he would not permit the demons to speak, because they knew him.

³⁵ In the morning, while it was still very dark, he got up and went out to a deserted place, and there he prayed. ³⁶ And Simon and his companions hunted for him. ³⁷ When they found him, they said to him, "Everyone is searching for you." ³⁸ He answered, "Let us go on to the neighboring towns, so that I may proclaim the message there also; for that is what I came out to do." ³⁹ And he went throughout Galilee, proclaiming the message in their synagogues and casting out demons.

Questions for a Closer Look

1 In verse 2, who seems to be speaking? Who is the "messenger"? Who is "you"?

2 Who speaks in verse 11?

3 Read verses 16–20, 29–30, and 35–38. What do they suggest about Jesus and his first followers? How well do his followers understand him?

4 What do Jesus' words and actions in this reading tell us about him?

A Guide to the Reading

Who is Jesus of Nazareth? Many of us would answer, "He is the Son of God." But who can fully understand what it means to be God's Son and how we should relate to him? Mark writes his Gospel to help fellow Christians better understand Jesus as "the Son of God" (1:1) and what it means to follow him.

John the Baptist is single-minded about what he wants to accomplish. He gets rid of all the comforts and pleasures of life so that he can focus on what he expects God to do (1:6–8). The way he lives his life is a lesson to us in opening the way for God to work in our lives. We must show that we really believe that whatever God wants to do is the most important thing in the world. We have to face up to our sins and seek God's forgiveness (1:4).

John's ministry is the beginning of the Good News of Jesus (1:1), and he can continue to open our lives to the Good News. John teaches us that for us to experience Jesus' coming, we must rid ourselves of all the things that keep us from responding to God's grace.

Jesus' first public act is to be baptized by John (1:9). God declares after the baptism that Jesus is his Son and that the Holy Spirit will give him the authority to do his work (1:10–11). Jesus is able to do his work because of his relationship with God. In the same way, our relationship with God enables us to do the work God has in mind for us.

Jesus returns to Galilee and announces that the time has come for God to take decisive action among us: "The kingdom of God has come near" (1:15). God is beginning to rule over us in a direct, liberating way. Like John, Jesus calls people to repent, but his message is slightly different. The message might be something like this: "Stop thinking and acting as though God were far from us, doing nothing. *God is on the move!* Change whatever you have to so that you can respond to him!"

When Jesus told us that God's reign "has come near," he wanted us to understand that God's Kingdom is now arriving but it has not yet arrived. We can see God's Kingdom, but it is still somewhat hidden. It takes faith to see God at work because God did not immediately set things right. Thus Jesus challenges people to *believe* in the good news of God's Kingdom, even though the kingdom is still somewhat hidden (1:15).

The first story that Mark tells is about Jesus calling his disciples. Jesus sets out to gather and train a group of followers so he can share his mission with them. Jesus does the same thing today, calling us to become his followers and join his other followers.

The fishermen that Jesus calls immediately leave their nets and boats—and even their father—and begin to walk along the lakeshore with him (1:16–20). They are not responding to just his message; they are also responding to his invitation to enter into a personal relationship with him.

In Mark's story of Jesus' sudden call to these men, we sense Jesus' personal authority over people. The next story Mark tells, about Jesus' teaching in the synagogue in Capernaum, further illustrates the uniqueness of Jesus' authority. People are amazed that Jesus teaches about God on his own authority rather than by referring to learned opinions, as other Jewish teachers did (1:21–22,27). The power of Jesus' teaching can be seen in the story of Jesus' confrontation with an evil spirit that is afflicting a man—probably with illness (1:23–26). When Jesus speaks, people are changed!

Mark mentions that Jesus heals Peter's mother-in-law (1:31). This episode is important because it shows us what it means to follow Jesus—being called, being healed, and beginning to serve. While who the mother-in-law is and what she does seem insignificant, that is exactly what makes her a good example of what Jesus expects from us.

Questions for Application

1 How do you think God helps people be more trusting in him and more open to his love?

2 If you knew that God was about to get directly involved in your life, what would you do to get ready?

3 What have you been taught about the importance of your Baptism in your relationship with God?

4 When do young people find it especially difficult to feel God's presence in their lives?

5 What are some ways in which you are serving others? What are some ways in which you are being served by others?

Approach to Prayer

Reflect for a moment on the story of Peter and Andrew leaving their nets and following Jesus when he called them. Then pray silently to Saints Peter and Andrew, asking their help in responding to Jesus' call. Do the same with the story of James and John. Reflect for a moment on James and John leaving their father and following Jesus when he called them, and then pray silently to them for their help in responding to Jesus' call.

Close the reflection time by praying this short prayer along with the group: "Lord, help each of us hear your call. Give us the grace to respond to you." End with the Our Father.

Saints in the Making

Life-giving Touch

Jesus touched and healed a man suffering from leprosy
(1:40–45). Because of his leprosy, the man had been shunned by
everyone else in society. Jesus' touch, therefore, not only made
the man well physically but also enabled him to have contact
with others.

Leprosy deforms the body terribly. People used to think that it
was very contagious, so they stayed away from the victims of
leprosy, regarding them as untouchable. But Christians have
always imitated Jesus by caring for men and women suffering
from leprosy. For some the simple act of touching a person
with leprosy has been a life-changing experience. Saint Francis
of Assisi was one of these people. The sight of leprosy filled him
with horror. If a leper approached him and asked for a
handout, Francis would give him a coin but avoid any physical
contact. One day, however, when a man with leprosy came up
to him, on a sudden inspiration Francis placed the coin in the
man's hand and then bent down and kissed his fingers. It was a
victory over self-protectiveness, which Francis followed up the
next day by visiting the local hospital for leprosy victims. Later
Francis wrote, "The Lord granted me to begin my conversion.
As long as I lived in my sins, I felt very bitter to see the lepers.
But the Lord took me among them, and I exercised mercy
towards them."

Closer to our own time was Father Damien, who spent much of
his life on the Hawaiian island of Molokai, caring for lepers and
eventually catching the disease himself. At first he was afraid to
touch them. But soon his love for them as people overcame his
fears, and he would wash them and dress their sores. As Pope
John Paul II declared in 1995 when beatifying Father Damien,
"He became a leper among the lepers; he became a leper for the

lepers." Damien touched their suffering bodies with his hands, but he also touched their souls with his beautiful spirituality.

Are we afraid of someone's pain? Are there suffering people whom we do not want to touch or even get close to? Will we let God help us to love them?

Between Discussions

The first chapter of Mark gives us a clear picture of God beginning to put into operation the plans he had made long before. We can almost feel the anticipation building in the description of John the Baptist's desert life and his preaching of repentance. Jesus announces that God's Kingdom is near, and the people he meets are immediately affected.

The coming of God's reign means that God is beginning to care for us in a new way. It also means that we are going to have to respond to God in a new way. If God were distant from us and not involved in our affairs, it might be enough if we only followed his general guidelines for living. But if God comes personally to free us from evil and reconcile us to him, we should answer him personally and completely.

God's action among us is not vague or abstract. It is actually something, or rather someone, we can touch: Jesus of Nazareth. It is in Jesus that God makes himself present. Thus the way to say yes to God is to say yes to Jesus. Mark illustrates his point in his story about the calling of the first disciples. Jesus invites Peter, Andrew, James, and John to follow him; they put everything aside so they can follow him. The story serves as a model of God's invitation and people's response.

Jesus' encounters with people troubled by "unclean spirits," or "demons," seem rather puzzling. People believed that illness was caused by the presence of evil spirits. Christians today recognize the existence of the devil and evil spirits, but we no longer see demons as a major source of sickness. So while we may not agree with those first-century people who blamed sickness on demons, we can believe that Jesus really did free people from physical and mental suffering. He showed that he could exercise God's power over all evils, material and spiritual. Indeed, he has power over all the evils that we ourselves will ever face. His casting out of demons signals that the final struggle between God and evil has begun.

John the Baptist encourages people to step into the Jordan River and receive a "baptism of repentance for the forgiveness of sins" (1:4). Their baptism is an expression of their sorrow for sins and their expectation of God's forgiveness. This expectation suggests to us that forgiveness will be a major part of what Jesus does, and indeed forgiveness comes to the fore in the next section of Mark.

Jesus heals a man of a skin disease that makes him ritually impure under the Jewish law (1:40–45). People regarded such a skin disease as a sign that the man was guilty of some sin, so Jesus' healing of the man is a symbol of forgiveness. Then Jesus tells a paralyzed man that his sins are forgiven (2:5). Finally, Jesus encounters a man whose occupation involves unjust practices and challenges him to become his disciple. Then he accepts an invitation to dinner at the man's home with some of his colleagues in injustice (2:13–17). Just by eating with them, Jesus seems to extend God's forgiveness to the man and his guests.

We can only understand Jesus' actions when we look at them against the background of what the Jews of his time expected—namely, that God would free all his people. When people see Jesus perform small acts of forgiveness and healing, they interpret them as signals that God is about to do great things that will impact the whole world. Yet Jesus acts in a way that goes beyond Jewish expectations. The rabbis wait for students to come to them, but Jesus calls disciples to him, as though he has the right to decide how people live their lives. He overpowers the forces of evil. He cures diseases with a word or a touch—with the power of the Creator. He does what only God has the authority to do: forgive sins. He brings people back to God through his own friendship with them, without their having to offer sacrifices in the Temple. The religious authorities saw Jesus' behavior as something like an invasion of God's territory and a threat to their law and the Temple in Jerusalem (2:7,16). He is heading towards a clash with these religious figures.

Who Is This Man?

Warm-Up Questions

1 What do you most enjoy doing on weekends?

2 Do young people sometimes have trouble communicating something important to their parents? How do you handle it when you have something important to tell your parents?

Opening the Bible

What's Happened

Jesus has begun to come into conflict with some of the Jewish religious leaders. In the process of healing a paralyzed man, Jesus tells him that his sins are forgiven. Some of the religious leaders wonder why he speaks in this way. "It is blasphemy! Who can forgive sins but God alone?" (2:7). Jesus gives them even more to wonder about when he goes on to speak and act as a friend and even a "physician" of sinners (2:13–17).

Jews living in the first century felt it was very important to keep the Sabbath, a practice that continues among the Jews of today. Observance of the Sabbath demonstrated one's loyalty to God and faithfulness to the people of Israel. Jews took different approaches to keeping the Sabbath, however, and sometimes criticized each other's approach. In our next reading Jesus enters this theological battlefield and takes a unique stand.

THE READING

Mark 2:23—3:35

Two Disputes

^{2:23} One sabbath he was going through the grainfields; and as they made their way his disciples began to pluck heads of grain. ²⁴ The Pharisees said to him, "Look, why are they doing what is not lawful on the sabbath?" ²⁵ And he said to them, "Have you never read what David did when he and his companions were hungry and in need of food? ²⁶ He entered the house of God, when Abiathar was high priest, and ate the bread of the Presence, which it is not lawful for any but the priests to eat, and he gave some to his companions." ²⁷ Then he said to them, "The sabbath was made for humankind, and not humankind for the sabbath; ²⁸ so the Son of Man is lord even of the sabbath."

^{3:1} Again he entered the synagogue, and a man was there who had a withered hand. ² They watched him to see whether he would cure him on the sabbath, so that they might accuse him. ³ And he said to the man who had the withered hand, "Come

forward." [4] Then he said to them, "Is it lawful to do good or to do harm on the sabbath, to save life or to kill?" But they were silent. [5] He looked around at them with anger; he was grieved at their hardness of heart and said to the man, "Stretch out your hand." He stretched it out, and his hand was restored. [6] The Pharisees went out and immediately conspired with the Herodians against him, how to destroy him.

Crowds, Followers, Opponents, and Family

[7] Jesus departed with his disciples to the sea, and a great multitude from Galilee followed him. . . . [9] He told his disciples to have a boat ready for him because of the crowd, so that they would not crush him; [10] for he had cured many, so that all who had diseases pressed upon him to touch him. . . .

[19] . . . Then he went home; [20] and the crowd came together again, so that they could not even eat. [21] When his family heard it, they went out to restrain him, for people were saying, "He has gone out of his mind." [22] And the scribes who came down from Jerusalem said, "He has Beelzebul, and by the ruler of the demons he casts out demons." [23] And he called them to him, and spoke to them in parables, "How can Satan cast out Satan? [24] If a kingdom is divided against itself, that kingdom cannot stand. [25] And if a house is divided against itself, that house will not be able to stand. [26] And if Satan has risen up against himself and is divided, he cannot stand, but his end has come. [27] But no one can enter a strong man's house and plunder his property without first tying up the strong man; then indeed the house can be plundered.

[28] "Truly I tell you, people will be forgiven for their sins and whatever blasphemies they utter; [29] but whoever blasphemes against the Holy Spirit can never have forgiveness, but is guilty of an eternal sin"—[30] for they had said, "He has an unclean spirit."

[31] Then his mother and his brothers came; and standing outside, they sent to him and called him. [32] A crowd was sitting around him; and they said to him, "Your mother and your brothers and sisters are outside, asking for you." [33] And he replied, "Who are my mother and my brothers?" [34] And looking at those who sat around him, he said, "Here are my mother and my brothers! [35] Whoever does the will of God is my brother and sister and mother."

Questions for a Closer Look

1 Do Jesus' opponents question his *ability* to heal?

2 Mark tells us in 3:21 that "people were saying, 'He has gone out of his mind.'" What would have prompted them to say such a thing?

3 To whom does *they* refer in 3:20?

4 Why do you think there is no mention of Jesus' father in 3:31–35?

A Guide to the Reading

The two incidents that begin our reading seem at first to be about disagreements over how to interpret the law prohibiting work on the Sabbath (2:23—3:6). But they are really about something more important, which is why they evoke such strong feelings during the discussions (3:5–6).

As they walk beside a field, Jesus' disciples pull off heads of grain and eat the raw seeds. The law allowed poor people to take food in this way (Leviticus 19:9–10; 23:22). Apparently Jesus' followers are poor. But they are doing it on the Sabbath, and some religious leaders, perhaps also out for a Sabbath stroll, accuse Jesus of letting his disciples break the law against harvesting on the Sabbath (2:23–24).

Jesus does not agree with the Pharisees' interpretation of the Sabbath law. He embarrasses them by pointing out that once the much-respected King David acted in a way in which the Pharisees would not have approved (2:25–26). The David incident shows that the Mosaic law allows for exceptions in order to meet the needs of hungry people.

But Jesus is not just arguing in favor of giving priority to human needs. He is also saying something about himself. He is comparing himself with David, Israel's greatest king, and he suggests that he has authority over one of Israel's basic institutions, the Sabbath.

The Pharisees also consider healing to be a form of work forbidden on the Sabbath (3:1–2). They recognize, as do all Jews, that one should break the Sabbath rules in order to save human life. But a shriveled hand is not life threatening, so why does Jesus speak in terms of life and death?

The answer is that Jesus *does* consider the man to be in a life-or-death situation. The Kingdom of God is coming into the world through Jesus' teaching and healing. For the man with the withered hand, meeting Jesus in the synagogue *is* a matter of life and death. If he receives healing from Jesus, he enters a new, living relationship with God; to miss the opportunity would be a kind of death. God's life-giving reign over human beings is coming through Jesus. What Jesus does, then, is more important than the rules for keeping the Sabbath.

Jesus makes two points in both these incidents. First, Sabbath rules should be applied in such a way that basic human needs can be met. Second, Jesus is God's agent in a way that takes precedence over other considerations. Significantly, the two points go together. Giving priority to people's needs and giving priority to Jesus go hand in hand.

People react in different ways to Jesus' healings and his claim that he plays a unique role in God's plans. His healing power attracts crowds (3:7,9–10,20), as might be expected, but at the same time many religious leaders take a stand against him. The religious leaders realize that if they do not stop Jesus, he will change the whole structure of Judaism. They believe that God wants things to stay the way they are, so they conclude that Jesus' powers come from the devil rather than from God (3:22).

Jesus defends himself by arguing that when he frees people from the effects of demons, it should be clear that he has overcome the demons' leader (3:27). Moreover, he says that to see the devil at work in what he does is to reject God's offer of reconciliation. Jesus is, after all, the one through whom God is overcoming evil and offering forgiveness. God is willing to forgive whatever sins anyone commits, but if we refuse the person through whom God offers forgiveness, we will remain alienated from God (3:29). The choice is ours.

Hearing that Jesus is deranged, some members of his family come to "restrain" him (3:20–21). In response Jesus declares that his real family members are those who obey God by following his teaching (3:31–35). The picture of people sitting around a room and listening to Jesus is a simple but profound image of the Church, the continuing community of Jesus' followers.

Questions for Application

1 In what different ways do we need healing?

2 What are some steps young people can take in order to serve Jesus in new ways? How can they fit what Jesus wants to do in their lives into their usual pattern of activities, habits, and preferences?

3 Do you sometimes regard your own concerns as more important than the needs of other people? What message does today's reading have for you in this regard?

4 Do people who give their whole lives and beings to Jesus sometimes seem a little crazy? Why?

5 Do you see your following of Jesus more as an individual thing or as something you do with other disciples? What do you do to express your belonging to the community of Jesus' followers?

Approach to Prayer

Listen as a member of the group reads Mark 3:7–10 aloud. After a minute of silence, if you wish, mention the names of relatives and friends who are sick, suffering, lonely, or having a hard time in life. Then recite this prayer with the group: "Lord Jesus, we bring all of these people to you, trusting in your love for them. Meet their needs, Lord. Guide us in helping to meet their needs also." End with the Our Father.

Saints in the Making

A Miraculous Cure

Jesus' remarkable cures were signs that God's reign was coming into the world. In every age of the Church, God has continued to provide such signs of the presence of his kingdom.

Some of these miracles occur because people pray to saints and ask for their help. At times Christians seek help from someone who has not yet been declared a saint. A miraculous answer can be taken as evidence that the person is in heaven. In fact, in considering whether to declare someone a saint, the Catholic Church requires at least one miraculous healing through the potential saint's intercession. A striking example of such an answer to prayer involved a little Massachusetts girl named Teresia Benedicta McCarthy. Her parents named her after Edith Stein, a German Jew who became a Christian and entered the Carmelite order as Sister Teresa Benedicta of the Cross. Edith Stein perished with a trainload of other Jews and people of Jewish ancestry in the gas chamber at Auschwitz death camp in August 1942.

In 1987 when Benedicta—as the little girl was known—was two years old, she swallowed a lethal dose of Acetaminophen. Her liver swelled up to five times its normal size and stopped functioning. Her kidneys began to fail. She continued to breathe only with the help of a machine. While the medical team began a nationwide search for a liver to transplant, Benedicta's parents decided to pray to Edith Stein. They called a couple of dozen friends and asked them to do the same. Within days Benedicta's liver and kidneys were functioning normally.

Doctors and theologians spent about 10 years going over the medical records and other details of Benedicta's recovery. In 1997 the Vatican announced that Benedicta's healing was indeed a miracle. By that time Benedicta was a healthy 12-year-old who did not remember her early brush with death. Since Benedicta's healing came after prayers for Edith Stein's intercession, the miracle fulfilled the requirement for her canonization. In October 1998 Pope John Paul II formally added Edith Stein to the list of saints recognized by the Church.

Between Discussions

Jesus' disciples must have been astonished at the way he acted and spoke. Here was an ordinary man, the carpenter of a nearby village, acting as though he had divine power over people's lives, over Jewish law and religion, over evil spirits. The Jews had not been prepared by their religion to expect God to act in such a way through a human agent; they had no one with whom to compare Jesus. Yet the disciples were convinced that the religious leaders were wrong about him (3:22). Jesus could not have received his power from the devil. It had to come from God because Jesus did the kinds of things you would expect from God's Spirit—reconciling people with God, restoring their physical and spiritual wholeness, bringing them peace.

In the chapters we skip (4:1—8:26), the disciples are shown struggling to understand who Jesus is. Mark tells how Jesus uses his extraordinary power to show people how God's Kingdom is arriving. He miraculously feeds thousands of hungry people. He cures diseases and calms a storm. He even raises someone from the dead. Meanwhile the disciples have trouble understanding what Jesus is about. Sometimes he seems to be what they expected; at other times he isn't at all what they expected. Jesus attracts and baffles them at the same time.

Like many Jews of the time, Jesus' followers probably expected that God would grant forgiveness and reconciliation to his people Israel. He would gather the scattered members of his people and dwell among them more openly in the Temple. He would restore them as a nation and give them prosperity, peace, and possession of their land.

When Jesus chose 12 of his followers to be an inner circle, it must have raised the disciples' hopes that Jesus was restoring Israel because Israel originally consisted of 12 tribes. Yet Jesus did nothing to drive the occupying Romans out of the land of Israel. It is important to note that among his apostles was a man who worked for the occupiers (Matthew, a former tax collector) and a man who fought for freedom from the occupiers (Simon the

Canaanaean—the title means "zealot" or "holy warrior"). Jesus, it seems, was promoting reconciliation among people rather than a political and economic program.

Many Jews thought that God's Kingdom would sweep away all injustice and suffering and open an entirely new age. They would have seen Jesus' miracles as powerful confirmation that God's Kingdom really was arriving. Yet Jesus taught his disciples that the new era of God's reign was beginning now, without getting rid of all the sin, injustice, and sorrow that exist in the world. In his parables he speaks of a kingdom that grows from small beginnings. Like a seed, it remains hidden for a time, then breaks into the open and bears fruit (chapter 4).

Mark shows that Jesus' disciples understand to some extent who he is and what he is about. They continue to share his life as they walk with him from town to town. When he sends them out to announce God's Kingdom, they carry out their commission (6:7–13). Yet they do not fully understand who he is. Even after witnessing one of his most amazing displays of power, Jesus has to ask them, "Do you not yet understand?" (8:21).

At the end of the section of Mark that we are skipping, Jesus performs an odd miracle. In two stages, he heals a man of blindness (8:22–26). At first the man recovers his sight partially. Jesus then puts his hands on the man's eyes again, and his sight is fully restored. The story is symbolic of Jesus' relationship with his disciples. They too need a miracle of healing to see who Jesus is and what it means to follow him. They too will receive their sight in stages. The next stage will occur in the incident we are about to read.

Turning Point

Warm-Up Questions

1 If you could have a conversation with someone famous or important, who would the person be and what would you talk about?

2 Are your first impressions of people usually reliable? Have you ever changed your opinion of someone after you have gotten to know him or her better?

Opening the Bible

What's Happened

Jesus has traveled with his disciples from place to place, mobbed by people seeking healing for themselves or their loved ones. The scope of his miracles has increased. He calms a storm (4:35–41). He brings peace to a man driven wild by inner conflict (5:1–13; the man is infested with a legion of demons, that is, six thousand demons!). He raises a little girl from the dead (5:35–43). Twice he feeds thousands of people with some fish and a few loaves of bread (6:33–44; 8:1–10). Nevertheless, the religious leaders remain unconvinced that he has been authorized by God (8:11–13).

THE READING

Mark 8:27—9:9

You Are the Messiah

8:27 Jesus went on with his disciples to the villages of Caesarea Philippi; and on the way he asked his disciples, "Who do people say that I am?" 28 And they answered him, "John the Baptist; and others, Elijah; and still others, one of the prophets." 29 He asked them, "But who do you say that I am?" Peter answered him, "You are the Messiah." 30 And he sternly ordered them not to tell anyone about him.

31 Then he began to teach them that the Son of Man must undergo great suffering, and be rejected by the elders, the chief priests, and the scribes, and be killed, and after three days rise again. 32 He said all this quite openly. And Peter took him aside and began to rebuke him. 33 But turning and looking at his disciples, he rebuked Peter and said, "Get behind me, Satan! For you are setting your mind not on divine things but on human things."

34 He called the crowd with his disciples, and said to them, "If any want to become my followers, let them deny themselves and take up their cross and follow me. 35 For those who want to save their life will lose it, and those who lose their life for my sake, and for the sake of the gospel, will save it. 36 For what will it profit

them to gain the whole world and forfeit their life? [37] Indeed, what can they give in return for their life? [38] Those who are ashamed of me and of my words in this adulterous and sinful generation, of them the Son of Man will also be ashamed when he comes in the glory of his Father with the holy angels." [9:1] And he said to them, "Truly I tell you, there are some standing here who will not taste death until they see that the kingdom of God has come with power."

This Is My Son

[2] Six days later, Jesus took with him Peter and James and John, and led them up a high mountain apart, by themselves. And he was transfigured before them, [3] and his clothes became dazzling white, such as no one on earth could bleach them. [4] And there appeared to them Elijah with Moses, who were talking with Jesus. [5] Then Peter said to Jesus, "Rabbi, it is good for us to be here; let us make three dwellings, one for you, one for Moses, and one for Elijah." [6] He did not know what to say, for they were terrified. [7] Then a cloud overshadowed them, and from the cloud there came a voice, "This is my Son, the Beloved; listen to him!" [8] Suddenly when they looked around, they saw no one with them any more, but only Jesus.

[9] As they were coming down the mountain, he ordered them to tell no one about what they had seen, until after the Son of Man had risen from the dead.

Questions for a Closer Look

1 How would you answer Jesus' question in 8:27: "Who do people say that I am"?

2 Why does Jesus speak so sharply to Peter?

3 What do you think Jesus meant when he talked to Peter about "setting your mind not on divine things but on human things" (8:33)?

4 What do you think prompted Jesus to issue his "order" in 9:9?

A Guide to the Reading

For some time Jesus' disciples have observed him at close range and have struggled to understand who he is. Now they have reached a conclusion: he is the Messiah, the one chosen by God to play the crucial role in the coming of God's Kingdom.

Jesus' disciples probably felt excited about reaching that conclusion about who he is. They can now look forward to watching him fulfill Jewish hopes for their nation. But they have just begun to understand who Jesus is and what his plans are; there is much more to learn. As soon as Peter declares who Jesus is, Jesus commands his followers not to discuss it with anyone (8:30). While their understanding of him is correct as far as it goes, it does not go far enough. Jesus *is* the Messiah. But they do not yet grasp what kind of messiah he is. They do not yet know that he is the Son of God or have any idea of the death by which he will accomplish his mission.

Jesus and his disciples have seen things differently, but their differences have not come out into the open until now. As soon as Jesus speaks about his approaching death (8:31), the differences explode into the open. Peter had spoken for the other disciples and declared Jesus the Messiah (8:29). Now he speaks for them again, objecting to Jesus' plans (8:32).

Jesus rebukes Peter sharply. When he says, "Get behind me, Satan!" (8:33), what he means is "Don't get in my way! If you're going to be my follower, then *follow* me!"

Yet Jesus' attitude toward his disciples is not harsh: he patiently teaches them (8:34–38). "If you are my disciple," Jesus says, "you must make a basic decision to let go of yourself and give your life to me." This is often taken to mean that Jesus' disciples should let go of things. But Jesus calls his disciples not to deny themselves *things* but to deny *themselves.* A figure skater who denied herself alcohol or tobacco while in training in order to win a competition would not be a model of self-denial. She might very well be an example of self-denial, however, if she dropped out of competition in order to care for her sick mother.

Up to this point in Mark's Gospel, it has probably been easy for most of us to identify with Jesus' disciples. They are like us, willing to follow Jesus and hopeful that it will make their lives better. Do we now continue to see ourselves in the disciples? Do we recognize ourselves in their failure to understand Jesus' plan to submit to a painful and humiliating death? Are we like them, thinking in an earthly way rather than in the way God thinks (see 8:33)? Jesus calls his followers to live for life in the age to come, when Jesus "comes in the glory of his Father" (8:38). Are we willing to live for that?

After this conversation, Jesus begins a journey to Jerusalem, where he knows he will die. The disciples will have to change the way they look at things if they are going to stay with him all the way to the cross. Do we also need to change the way we look at things, if we are to go where Jesus wants to lead us?

The disciples have not understood that Jesus will die a terrible death, nor have they understood his divine sonship. On the subject of his sonship, they will now receive an extraordinary revelation. Three of his closest followers are given a vision of Jesus radiant with heavenly light, standing with the two greatest prophets of Israel. The vision reveals to the terrified disciples (9:6) that Jesus is much greater than they supposed. Jesus has puzzled friends, family, and foes by acting with a more-than-human authority. The voice of God now proclaims what has only been hinted at before: Jesus is God's Son.

It is important to note that this vision does not occur right after Peter acknowledges Jesus as Messiah; it happens only after Jesus explains the kind of messianic mission he is on and what it will require of his followers (8:31–38). Thus when God commands the disciples to pay attention to Jesus (9:7), he confirms Jesus' words about his death and about taking up one's cross to follow him.

Questions for Application

1 When have you had a moment of coming to know Jesus in a deeper way? What is something a young person can do to know Jesus better?

2 What are some things that would be hard for you to let go of? Do you think Jesus was serious about us denying ourselves?

3 How is a young person, who is thinking of a good career and a good life, supposed to apply what Jesus said in 8:36?

4 God strengthens the disciples' faith in Jesus by giving them a vision of Jesus' divine glory. What have others done to build your faith in Jesus? How might you strengthen the faith of other people?

5 God tells the disciples to listen to Jesus (9:7). What are some things that get in the way of our listening to Jesus? What could we do to reduce the interference?

Approach to Prayer

Listen as a member of the group reads Mark 9:2–8 aloud. Pause for silent reflection. Pray along silently as a group member reads aloud this Eastern Christian prayer:

Before your crucifixion, O Lord,
taking the disciples up into a
high mountain, you were transfigured
before them, shining on them
with the bright beams of
your power. From love of
humankind you desired to show them
the splendor of the resurrection.
Grant that we too in peace may be counted
worthy of this splendor, O God, for you are
merciful and love humankind.

End by praying together the Our Father.

A Living Tradition

Denial of Self

In 2001 Pope John Paul II sent a World Youth Day message to the young people of the world. He chose as his theme the message of Jesus which we encountered in today's reading from Mark: we must deny ourselves and follow Jesus in carrying the cross. The Holy Father ended his message with these words:

My dear young people, do not think it strange that, at the beginning of the third millennium, the Pope once again directs you towards the Cross of Christ as the path of life and true happiness. The Church has always believed and proclaimed that only in the Cross of Christ is there salvation.

There is a widespread culture of the ephemeral that only attaches value to whatever is pleasing or beautiful, and it would like us to believe that it is necessary to remove the cross in order to be happy. The ideal presented is one of instant success, a fast career, sexuality separated from any sense of responsibility, and ultimately, an existence centred on self affirmation, often bereft of respect for others.

Open your eyes and observe well, my dear young people: this is not the road that leads to true life, but it is the path that sinks into death. Jesus said: 'Whoever wishes to save his life will lose it, but whoever loses his life for my sake will save it.' Jesus leaves us under no illusions: 'What profit is there for one to gain the whole world yet lose or forfeit himself?' (Luke 9:24–25). With the truth of his words that sound hard but fill the heart with peace, Jesus reveals the secret of how to live a true life.

Therefore, do not be afraid to walk the way first trodden by the Lord. With your youthfulness, put your mark of hope and enthusiasm, so typical of your age, on the third millennium that is just beginning. If you allow the grace of

God to work in you, and earnestly fulfill this commitment daily, you will make this new century a better time for everyone.

Mary the Mother of the Lord always walks with you. She was the first of the disciples, and she remained faithful at the foot of the Cross where Christ entrusted us to her motherly care. May this Apostolic Blessing that I impart with great affection be with you always.

Between Discussions

Jesus' ministry and his dealings with his disciples now enter a new phase. The disciples are like the blind man healed at Bethsaida (8:22–26): they are beginning to see, but not all at once. They recognize Jesus as the Messiah, but they are just starting to understand that Jesus is God's Son and what it will mean to follow him.

After the conversation about who Jesus is and the revelation on the mountain, Jesus begins a journey south to Jerusalem. On this trip Jesus' focus shifts. Up to now, his miracles have signaled the coming of the Kingdom. Now he works fewer miracles and focuses instead on teaching his disciples how to respond to the coming of God's Kingdom. His Kingdom is different than they expect and they are going to have to respond differently than they have so far.

Once again Jesus takes up the subject of his approaching death (9:30–31). But his disciples do not understand because right away they start arguing over which of them has the most important role in Jesus' plans (9:34). They don't yet understand that living in God's Kingdom is more about love for other people than self-promotion (see 9:35–37).

Jesus teaches them about relationships among his followers and about marriage, children, and material resources (9:38—10:31). Then he returns once more to the subject of his impending death and resurrection (10:32–34). Still his disciples do not understand. Two of them immediately ask him to appoint them to the most important positions of authority in his kingdom (10:35–37). The two disciples address Jesus as "Teacher" (10:35). Yet rather than learning from him, they seem intent on getting him to do what they want. If they regarded Jesus as their teacher, they would be more willing to do whatever *he* asks.

In response Jesus tells them that true greatness does not lie in having authority over people but in caring for them (10:42–44). Jesus tells them in 10:45 to serve—the Greek word literally means "to wait on tables." He says that he himself is this kind of servant.

The kind of service to which Jesus refers is ordinary; there is nothing grand, heroic or dramatic about it. The only person in Mark's Gospel besides Jesus who offers this kind of service is Peter's mother-in-law (1:31).

Jesus' words help answer an important question about how we can live as his disciples. Being a disciple of Jesus means more than accepting his teaching. A disciple of Jesus is invited to become his personal follower. Yet what can this mean for us, since it is impossible for us to literally follow Jesus as he travels from place to place?

The "territory" through which we can now follow Jesus is not Palestine but our own lives. We travel with him not from Caesarea Philippi to Jerusalem but from birth to death. How can we follow Jesus through this territory? How do we know which "roads" he is leading us on, where he wishes us to go, what he wishes us to do? We know that he calls us to die to ourselves and follow him, but how can we know concretely what that means here and now?

Part of the answer lies in Jesus' lesson about taking the place of least importance and serving others. We may all travel different paths, but they all lead through humble service. Thus we will have the best chance of finding the right path for our lives, the path Jesus wishes us to walk with him, if we take advantage of opportunities to serve other people. Of course, this will not answer all our questions about what path we should take. But if we are actively serving other people, we will at least be moving in the right direction and can trust Jesus to help us keep moving in that direction.

Finally, Jesus heals another blind man (10:46–52). This man's sight is restored all at once. Unlike other people whom Jesus heals, this man becomes one of Jesus' disciples. The significance of this miracle is hard to miss. The disciples may still be blind to Jesus' path of humble service, death to self, and resurrection, but he has the power to open their eyes and enable them—and us—to follow him.

The Hour Has Come

Warm-Up Questions

1 What is your favorite place to pray? Where do you feel most at peace?

2 What is the next important meal (holiday, family celebration, and so on) that you are looking forward to? What will everybody do to make it a happy occasion?

Opening the Bible

What's Happened

By coming to Jerusalem, Jesus provokes the religious authorities by a dramatic action that symbolizes the end of the Temple's usefulness. He further angers them with his teaching (11:15–19; 11:27—12:44).

Jews in the first century gathered at Passover, as do Jews today, to share a meal celebrating the Exodus—God's rescue of the Israelites from slavery in Egypt. In Jesus' day, Jews traveled to Jerusalem to have a sheep or a goat slaughtered in the Temple and then to eat the festive meal in the holy city. Jesus and his disciples share this meal on the night before his death (14:12–25).

THE READING

Mark 14:17–50

The Final Meal

14:17 When it was evening, he came with the twelve. 18 And when they had taken their places and were eating, Jesus said, "Truly I tell you, one of you will betray me, one who is eating with me." 19 They began to be distressed and to say to him one after another, "Surely, not I?" 20 He said to them, "It is one of the twelve, one who is dipping bread into the bowl with me. 21 For the Son of Man goes as it is written of him, but woe to that one by whom the Son of Man is betrayed! It would have been better for that one not to have been born."

22 While they were eating, he took a loaf of bread, and after blessing it he broke it, gave it to them, and said, "Take; this is my body." 23 Then he took a cup, and after giving thanks he gave it to them, and all of them drank from it. 24 He said to them, "This is my blood of the covenant, which is poured out for many. 25 Truly I tell you, I will never again drink of the fruit of the vine until that day when I drink it new in the kingdom of God."

26 When they had sung the hymn, they went out to the Mount of Olives. 27 And Jesus said to them, "You will all become deserters; for it is written,

'I will strike the shepherd,
        and the sheep will be scattered.'
[28] But after I am raised up, I will go before you to Galilee." [29] Peter said to him, "Even though all become deserters, I will not."
[30] Jesus said to him, "Truly I tell you, this day, this very night, before the cock crows twice, you will deny me three times." [31] But he said vehemently, "Even though I must die with you, I will not deny you." And all of them said the same.

An Anguished Prayer

[32] They went to a place called Gethsemane; and he said to his disciples, "Sit here while I pray." [33] He took with him Peter and James and John, and began to be distressed and agitated. [34] And he said to them, "I am deeply grieved, even to death; remain here, and keep awake." [35] And going a little farther, he threw himself on the ground and prayed that, if it were possible, the hour might pass from him. [36] He said, "Abba, Father, for you all things are possible; remove this cup from me; yet, not what I want, but what you want." [37] He came and found them sleeping; and he said to Peter, "Simon, are you asleep? Could you not keep awake one hour? [38] Keep awake and pray that you may not come into the time of trial; the spirit indeed is willing, but the flesh is weak." [39] And again he went away and prayed, saying the same words. [40] And once more he came and found them sleeping, for their eyes were very heavy; and they did not know what to say to him. [41] He came a third time and said to them, "Are you still sleeping and taking your rest? Enough! The hour has come; the Son of Man is betrayed into the hands of sinners. [42] Get up, let us be going. See, my betrayer is at hand."

[43] Immediately, while he was still speaking, Judas, one of the twelve, arrived; and with him there was a crowd with swords and clubs, from the chief priests, the scribes, and the elders. [44] Now the betrayer had given them a sign, saying, "The one I will kiss is the man; arrest him and lead him away under guard." [45] So when he came, he went up to him at once and said, "Rabbi!" and kissed him. [46] Then they laid hands on him and arrested him. . . . [48] Then Jesus said to them, "Have you come out with swords and clubs to arrest me as though I were a bandit? [49] Day after day I was with you in the temple teaching, and you did not arrest me. But let the scriptures be fulfilled." [50] All of them deserted him and fled.

Questions for a Closer Look

1 What does this reading tell you about Jesus' attitude toward the death that awaits him?

2 What indications does Jesus give that he is acting in accord with God's plan?

3 In Gethsemane Jesus keeps the same three disciples with him who saw him transfigured (9:2; 14:33). What do you think this means?

4 There is a lot of body language—gestures, postures—in this reading. How does it enrich the meaning?

A Guide to the Reading

During the Passover meal, Jesus takes bread and wine and shares them with his disciples as his own body and blood (14:22–24). He does this to link the meal with his death, showing the disciples that his death will be like the Passover: through it, God will bring liberation and life. The death he is about to undergo will, he says, create a "covenant" (14:24), restoring the broken relationship between God and human beings.

Jesus blessed and shared the cup of wine at the Passover meal. Earlier he had spoken of drinking a cup and of giving his life as a "ransom" (10:38–39,45). Drinking a cup of wine is used in Scripture as a metaphor for suffering punishment for sins (Isaiah 51:17; Jeremiah 49:12; Ezekiel 23:31–34). Jesus meant that he would pay the price of our sins. He would die so that others might live. In the Gospel of Matthew, Jesus makes the meaning clearer by saying that his blood is shed "for the forgiveness of sins" (Matthew 26:28). Nailed to a cross, Jesus will suffer the punishment that weighs on all sinners—his disciples, his family, his detractors, and us—so that they may be forgiven and changed.

Jesus believes that his death will bring God's Kingdom without delay, and this is what he means when he declares, "I will never again drink of the fruit of the vine until that day when I drink it new in the kingdom of God" (14:25).

When we celebrate the Eucharist, Jesus shares with us what he did in his final Passover meal and on the cross. Our sins are removed, and our relationship, our covenant, with God is renewed. We feast already in God's Kingdom. We are still awaiting the complete coming of God's Kingdom, but it has already begun to arrive through Jesus' death and resurrection. We experience it in part as we sit at table with the risen Lord.

One of the men eating the Passover meal with Jesus has been plotting to betray him (14:18–21). Other men celebrating the Passover across town will gather after their meal to arrest Jesus. Jesus is fully aware of all this as he leads the singing of the traditional psalms to end the Passover meal and goes out to meet the men who will kill him.

Along the way, Jesus tells his followers that they will soon abandon him (14:27). Peter grants that the other disciples may well do such a shameful thing (14:29). He is willing to believe that his fellow disciples are cowards—but he will not believe that he is. But Jesus knows Peter better than Peter does.

As usual, Jesus is realistic about his followers, not harsh. He looks beyond their upcoming failure and assures them of his resurrection (14:28). They will see him again. The Old Testament prophecy that Jesus quotes (14:27; Zechariah 13:7) reinforces the message that he is about to suffer the divine judgment for sins so that men and women may go free.

The garden of Gethsemane, on a hillside facing Jerusalem, is a place of decision for Jesus—and for the disciples. Jesus deliberately passes up his last chance to escape. His prayer gives us an idea of how hard it was for him to make this decision (14:36). The disciples have been warned that they are about to face a test of their loyalty to Jesus, yet they fail to turn to God for help (14:37,40–41). They have heard Jesus' message of the suffering entailed in following him, but they have not accepted it.

Nevertheless, Jesus continues to associate his followers with himself, speaking in terms of "us" right up to the moment they run away from him (14:42). He does not close the door to friendship with him, no matter how long it takes us to respond.

Jesus uses the term "be at hand" or "come near," this time to describe the approach of his betrayer (14:42; see 1:15). God's Kingdom will now indeed come, but in a way that no human being could have conceived: through his Son's arrest, rejection, torture, death, and resurrection.

Questions for Application

1 In Gethsemane Jesus must have felt as though God was almost asking too much of him. Have you ever felt that way? What is the best way to handle these situations?

2 What are some ways in which young people experience weakness in obeying God and a need for his help? What will help them overcome their weakness?

3 How do you feel when people ignore your advice? How do you respond to friends when they let you down? How do you go about setting things right after you have let down one of your friends?

4 Go back over the reading carefully, paying close attention to the picture of Jesus it paints. What should this picture of Jesus mean for your relationship with him?

5 In what ways do we all need to "keep awake," as Jesus urges in 14:34?

6 What can we do to be more receptive to Jesus in the celebration of the Eucharist?

Approach to Prayer

Listen as a member of the group reads Mark 14:36 aloud.
Then if you wish, voice the name of someone you know who is
in the midst of suffering of some kind.

Then pray Psalm 13 together.

> How long, O LORD? Will you forget
> me for ever?
>> How long will you hide your face
>> from me?
> How long must I bear pain in my
> soul,
>> and have sorrow in my heart all day
>> long?
> How long shall my enemy be exalted
> over me?
>
> Consider and answer me, O Lord, my
> God!
>> Give light to my eyes, or I will sleep
>> the sleep of death,
> And my enemy will say, 'I have
> prevailed';
>> my foes will rejoice because I am
>> shaken.
>
> But I trusted in your steadfast love;
>> my heart shall rejoice in your
>> salvation.
> I will sing to the LORD,
>> because he has dealt bountifully
>> with me.

Close by praying the Our Father with the group.

A Living Tradition

Children and the Eucharist

Saint Pius X was pope from 1903 to 1914. For centuries, it was the custom for Catholics to receive Communion only on special occasions, and children were not allowed to receive Communion at all. Pope Pius X changed all that. He advised all Catholics to receive Holy Communion frequently, if possible, daily, and he dispensed the sick from the obligation of fasting so that they could receive Holy Communion at least twice a month.

Pius X also lowered the age at which children could receive Communion. The story is told that one day an English lady brought her four-year-old son with her for a private visit with the pope. Pius X bent down to the little boy and asked him how old he was. "I am four," said the boy. When the pope asked him whom he received in Holy Communion, the boy answered, "Jesus Christ." "And who is Jesus Christ?" asked the pope. The boy responded, "Jesus Christ is God." With that, Pius X turned to the mother and said: "Bring your boy to me tomorrow and I will give him his first Communion myself."

In the document allowing younger children to receive Communion, Pius X wrote:

> *The pages of the Gospel show clearly how special was that love for children which Christ showed while He was on earth. It was His delight to be in their midst; He was wont to lay His hands on them; He embraced them; and He blessed them. At the same time He was not pleased when they would be driven away by the disciples, whom He rebuked gravely with these words: 'Let the little children come to me, and do not hinder them, for of such is the kingdom of God.' It is clearly seen how highly He held their innocence and the open simplicity of their souls on that occasion when He called a little child to Him and said to the*

disciples: 'Amen, I say to you, unless you turn and become like little children, you will not enter into the kingdom of heaven. . . . And whoever receives one such little child for my sake, receives me.'

Between Discussions

In the spring of 1535, Sir Thomas More, former chief administrator of the English government, sat in a cell in the royal prison called the Tower of London. King Henry VIII had jailed More for publicly refusing to support Henry's claim that, as king, he had the authority to govern the Church in England. The two men were old friends, but Henry was not a monarch to be crossed. More had every reason to expect to be executed for insisting that the pope, not the king, was the head of the Church in England.

With death before him, More turned his thoughts to Jesus' preparations for suffering. Over several weeks More wrote a commentary on the Gospel accounts of Jesus in the garden of Gethsemane that he entitled *Concerning the Sorrow, Weariness, Fear, and Prayer of Christ before His Arrest*. More did not live to complete the work. The manuscript breaks off abruptly—probably on June 12, 1535, the day prison authorities removed his paper and pens. Less than a month later, More's head fell under the executioner's ax.

In his commentary More pictured the moment when Jesus uttered the anguished words "I am deeply grieved, even to death" (14:34). Jesus sensed, More said, that he was about to face his betrayer, his accusers, the chains, the false charges, the verbal abuse, the scourging, the thorns, the nails, the cross, and the awful torture continuing hour after hour. It pained Jesus to think of the terror of his disciples, the ruin of the Jews, the death of his betrayer, and the anguish of his beloved mother. The thought of all these terrible things weighed heavily on his kind and gentle heart.

Why, More asked, did Jesus experience such fear, when he had taught his disciples not to be afraid (4:40; 6:50)? Why was he so afraid of the suffering that lay ahead of him (14:36) rather than set a "good example" of fearless bravery?

The answer, it seemed to More, is that Jesus' command not to be afraid hardly meant that his followers "should never in any way be afraid of a violent death. Rather they should not fear and flee a temporary kind of death in such a way that they would, by denying their faith, run into an eternal death." Since fear in the face of danger is prudent, More reasoned, Jesus' injunction against fear did not mean "never feel afraid" but "do not give way to fear out of lack of trust in God."

More thought that we should not turn away from suffering when it must be borne, but he also thought that we should not feel guilty about our dread of it. "There is no guilt attached to the fear of death and pain. In fact, this fear is an affliction that Christ came to suffer, not to escape." Fear is part of the human condition that the Son of God came to share with us.

More noted that while some people are naturally brave, many of us are not. Knowing this, Jesus encourages us "by the example of his own anguish, his own sadness, his own weariness, and his own unequaled fear." More imagined Jesus saying to those who are experiencing fear, "Take courage and do not lose hope. You are afraid; you are sad; you are stricken with weariness and agitated with fear of the torment that is cruelly directed toward you. Trust me. I have conquered the world, yet I was immeasurably more frightened, more saddened, more wearied, more terrified at the sight of such awful suffering approaching. Let the brave one rejoice to imitate a thousand courageous martyrs. But you, my timid and peace-loving little sheep, be content to have me as your only shepherd, to follow me as your leader. Since you do not have confidence in yourself, hope in me. Look, I am walking ahead of you on this frightening road."

For Thomas More in his prison cell, Jesus' fear and prayer in Gethsemane were immediately relevant. Unlike More, perhaps few of us will have to decide between a painful death and disloyalty to Christ. But we all meet situations in which the opportunity—or even the obligation—of service entails suffering, as well as situations in which suffering is simply thrust upon us. When our path leads through Gethsemane, More encourages us to draw close to Jesus, whom we will find there.

Messiah and Son of God

Warm-Up Questions

1 Has a teacher ever given you a second chance to do an assignment? How did it turn out?

2 Have you ever discovered that a situation was different from the way it seemed at first? How did you adjust?

Opening the Bible

Mark 14:53–72

Jesus Declares His Identity

14:53 They took Jesus to the high priest; and all the chief priests, the elders, and the scribes were assembled. 54 Peter had followed him at a distance, right into the courtyard of the high priest; and he was sitting with the guards, warming himself at the fire. 55 Now the chief priests and the whole council were looking for testimony against Jesus to put him to death; but they found none. 56 For many gave false testimony against him, and their testimony did not agree. 57 Some stood up and gave false testimony against him, saying, 58 "We heard him say, 'I will destroy this temple that is made with hands, and in three days I will build another, not made with hands.'" 59 But even on this point their testimony did not agree. 60 Then the high priest stood up before them and asked Jesus, "Have you no answer? What is it that they testify against you?" 61 But he was silent and did not answer. Again the high priest asked him, "Are you the Messiah, the Son of the Blessed One?" 62 Jesus said, "I am; and

'you will see the Son of Man
seated at the right hand of the Power,'
and 'coming with the clouds of heaven.'"

63 Then the high priest tore his clothes and said, "Why do we still need witnesses? 64 You have heard his blasphemy! What is your decision?" All of them condemned him as deserving death. 65 Some began to spit on him, to blindfold him, and to strike him, saying to him, "Prophesy!" The guards also took him over and beat him.

Peter Fails the Test

66 While Peter was below in the courtyard, one of the servant-girls of the high priest came by. 67 When she saw Peter warming himself, she stared at him and said, "You also were with Jesus, the man from Nazareth." 68 But he denied it, saying, "I do not know or understand what you are talking about." And he went out into the

forecourt. Then the cock crowed. [69] And the servant-girl, on seeing him, began again to say to the bystanders, "This man is one of them." [70] But again he denied it. Then after a little while the bystanders again said to Peter, "Certainly you are one of them; for you are a Galilean." [71] But he began to curse, and he swore an oath, "I do not know this man you are talking about." [72] At that moment the cock crowed for the second time. Then Peter remembered that Jesus had said to him, "Before the cock crows twice, you will deny me three times." And he broke down and wept.

Questions for a Closer Look

1 Mark tells us about Jesus' trial (14:55–65) right in the middle of telling us about Peter's betrayal (14:54,66–72). By doing it that way, what do you think he is trying to tell us about Jesus and Peter?

2 Reread what Mark says about Peter (14:27–31,33–41, 50,54,66–72). How would you describe Peter? What are his motivations? his strengths and weaknesses?

3 How would you explain the difference between Peter's self-confidence (14:29,31) and his later performance (14:67–71)?

A Guide to the Reading

Never have participants in an event been so blind to what is really taking place. The religious leaders see Jesus as a fraud and a troublemaker. They are absolutely sure that he is not the Messiah and Son of God, so all they do is get him to say that he is and they have enough evidence to convict him (14:61–63). They think that once they humiliate and execute him, everyone will see him as an imposter and forget about him. But they are wrong on both counts. He is right about being the Messiah and Son of God. And it is precisely by suffering torture and execution that he will fulfill his role as Messiah and Son of God.

False witnesses report that Jesus said he would destroy and rebuild the Temple (14:57–58). This testimony may be a garbled form of a statement that Jesus actually made about replacing the Jerusalem Temple with a new temple—the community of his followers. The accusers do not realize that their accusation, by helping to bring about Jesus' death, will contribute to the fulfillment of his prediction. Jesus' death and resurrection will establish a new bond between God and human beings. The men and women drawn into this relationship will offer God a deeper, more intimate worship in the community of the Church, the temple.

Tormentors mock Jesus as a false prophet for foretelling his eventual victory (14:65; see 14:62) at the very moment when Peter is fulfilling Jesus' prophecy of his betrayal (14:66–72; see 14:30). What they do not realize is that their abuse of him is helping bring about the fulfillment of God's plan that Jesus predicted: "And they will mock him, spit upon him, scourge him, and kill him, but after three days he will rise"(10:34). Mark's readers can see the irony in this situation, and it assures them that Jesus' prophecies that he will rise from the dead and form a new worshiping community will be fulfilled.

Jesus is not the kind of messiah the religious leaders envision. His Father's plan to use his suffering and death is different from any conception they have of God's action in the world. They do not see things from God's perspective; they see from a limited, purely human perspective (like Peter—8:33). We too suffer this limited perspective whenever we think that God's Kingdom does not require us to forgive people who hurt us, or to suffer in the service of others, or to speak the truth courageously.

People fail to perceive God's Kingdom, and in their ignorance even seek to destroy it. But in spite of this, God advances his purposes. Jesus endures the attacks of those who oppose him, and in that way opens the way for the coming of God's reign over human beings. It is not easy to see God's Kingdom coming, in part because it comes through the suffering of self-giving love.

Meanwhile, Peter has come to the house where the interrogation is being conducted. His relationship with Jesus is coming unraveled now that it has become dangerous to be associated with Jesus: Peter follows "at a distance" (14:54). This man, who has had the privilege of being with Jesus, now denies that he was with him (3:14; 14:67–71). The man who considered himself the bravest among Jesus' followers is too great a coward to acknowledge even belonging to the group (14:29,70–71). The man who claimed to know Jesus now protests that he does not know him (8:29; 14:71)—and, in a sense, he is right. Peter does not really know Jesus, the suffering Son of God, nor does he grasp the self-denial involved in following him.

The contrast between Jesus and Peter is striking. Jesus courageously affirms that he is God's Son, accepting the death that this declaration will bring. Peter, however, is too afraid to acknowledge who he is—a disciple of Jesus. In denying Jesus, Peter also denies himself.

Questions for Application

1 Compare Peter's behavior in Gethsemane (14:37,40–41) with his behavior in the priest's courtyard (14:66–72)? What can you learn from his behavior?

2 Peter is afraid to stay close to Jesus in his time of danger and suffering, so he only follows at a distance. What can a young person do to follow Jesus closely rather than at a distance?

3 Peter wept, obviously feeling guilty. When are feelings of guilt good for us, and when are they not good for us?

4 Jesus based his life on who he was in God's eyes—his Son. Who are you in God's eyes? How does that knowledge affect the way you live your life?

Approach to Prayer

Take time to pray for each other's needs. Begin by praying along silently as a member of the group reads aloud Psalm 4.

Answer when I call, O God of my
  right!
    You gave me room when I was in
    distress.
    Be gracious to me, and hear my
    prayer.

How long, you people, shall my
  honour suffer shame?
    How long will you love vain words,
    and seek after lies?

But know that the LORD has set apart
  the faithful for himself;
    the LORD hears when I call to him.

When you are disturbed, do not sin;
  ponder it on your beds, and be
  silent.
Offer right sacrifices,
  and put your trust in the LORD.

There are many who say, 'O that we
  might see some good!
    Let the light of your face shine on
    us, O LORD!'
You have put gladness in my heart
  more than when their grain and
  wine abound.

I will both lie down and sleep in
  peace;
    for you alone, O LORD, make me lie
    down in safety.

If you wish, mention briefly a need in your own life or in someone else's life. Reflect silently for a moment on your need for God's love and forgiveness. End by praying the Our Father together.

Saints in the Making

Are You One of This Man's Followers?

The servant came up to Peter in the courtyard and made a simple observation: "You also were with Jesus, the man from Nazareth" (14:67). She was not asking Peter to tell her all about Jesus or to give her proof that Jesus was the Messiah. The servant was merely challenging Peter to confirm something about himself, something she was already pretty sure of—that Peter was a follower of Jesus. He should have answered her by simply saying, "That's right."

From time to time, we too must stand up as followers of Jesus. We might have to tell someone that we believe in him or we might have to make a tough decision to do what we know is right. At such a time we face the same choice Peter faced: are we willing to speak and act in a way that shows everyone that we have a relationship with Jesus?

Sometimes people think they are prepared to live out their commitment to Jesus, and then they suddenly find out, as Peter did, that it is not so easy. On the other hand, there are people who don't consider themselves heroes, and yet in a crisis they rise to the occasion. In July 1941 there was an escape from Block 14 of the Auschwitz death camp in southern Poland. The men from the block were taken outside and made to stand all day without food or drink while the guards looked for the escapee. When it was clear that he would not be found, 10 prisoners were chosen to die in reprisal for the one prisoner's escape. One of these prisoners was a young man with a wife and children. The young man begged to be spared because his family would not survive without him, and Maximilian Kolbe, a Catholic priest from Poland, stepped forward and offered to be killed in his place. Father Kolbe was put in an underground starvation bunker, where he survived for two weeks until the guards killed him with a lethal dose of poison. Maximilian Kolbe came to be known as the Saint of Auschwitz, and he was canonized by Pope John Paul II in 1982.

Of course, we rarely face such life-threatening situations. Our choices usually involve far less-severe consequences. But in one way or another, all of us encounter challenges to affirm our relationship with Jesus. The example of people like Peter and Maximilian Kolbe leads us to examine ourselves and to reflect on Jesus' warnings about the price we might sometimes have to pay for our faith.

Between Discussions

I n our final excerpt from Mark, we will read about Jesus' death. As we all know, Jesus died on a cross. But Mark says little about the actual manner of Jesus' death (see 15:24), partly because it was shameful and partly because his readers did not need a description. Crucifixion was far from unusual in the Roman Empire, and it was always carried out in public. Consequently, many people had the opportunity to see crucifixion for themselves.

Mark and the other New Testament writers are quiet about the particulars of Jesus' death, so there is no way to reconstruct it as it actually was. But on the basis of ancient writings and archaeological discoveries, it is possible to get a picture of crucifixion that aids our reading of Mark.

In the first-century Roman world, crucifixion was considered the worst form of execution because it was extremely painful and often very slow. The victim was attached to a board or a stake, with or without a crosspiece, usually by nails through the feet and wrists (not through the hands, for the hands would pull loose of the nails). The atrocious pain of the body's weight bearing down on the nails was constantly intensified as the victim attempted to pull himself—or herself—up in order to breathe. Since no vital organs were directly involved, the crucified person might suffer for days before dying from dehydration and asphyxiation. A peg was sometimes supplied as a seat that enabled the victim to continue breathing, thereby prolonging the agony.

Usually the victim was flogged before being nailed to the cross. Often this punishment was a scourging—a lashing with whips tipped with bits of metal. The ferocity of scourging can be judged from the fact that some victims died from it. Such torture could hardly be called merciful, but by weakening the victim, it could shorten the time he would suffer on the cross before dying.

Crucifixion was designed as a deterrent and so was carried out where people could see it. The Romans crucified their victims along roads or, if they were besieging a city, outside the city walls as a message to the defenders about what awaited them if they did not surrender immediately.

Numerous details in the Gospel accounts of Jesus' death fit with the historical evidence concerning crucifixion. Mark tells us that when the execution squad led Jesus out to the place of crucifixion, they forced a man named Simon to carry the cross (15:20–21). It was common to make the victim himself carry the crosspiece to the place of execution. Apparently Jesus' scourging had been so severe, however, that he was too weak to do this. After Jesus' death, a member of the Jewish ruling council asked Pilate for Jesus' body for burial. Pilate was surprised that Jesus was dead so soon (15:44). His surprise fits with what we know about crucifixion as a usually prolonged agony, and it strengthens the conclusion that Jesus' scourging was especially terrible, bringing about a relatively rapid death.

Mark reports that "those who passed by" mocked Jesus (15:29). Jesus' cross was not set up on a lonely hill but along one of the roads into Jerusalem, probably just outside one of the city gates. The crucified person, stripped of all clothing and hanging in agony, was a public spectacle of utter humiliation.

The Gospel writer John reports that since Jesus was already dead, the soldiers did not break his legs, although they broke the legs of the other men crucified beside him (John 19:31–33). The practice of speeding up the crucified victim's death by breaking his legs, making it impossible for him to breathe, was illustrated by the 1968 discovery of the bones of a young Jewish man who had been crucified near Jerusalem in the first century. His lower leg bones had been shattered, apparently, in the view of the archaeologists and a medical examiner, in the manner that John describes in his Gospel.

The Ransom Is Given

Warm-Up Questions

1 Why is it sometimes better to remain silent after someone criticizes you or accuses you of something?

2 Describe a time when you were especially glad to have finished something on which you were working.

Opening the Bible

Mark 15:1–41

Crucify Him!

[15:1] As soon as it was morning, the chief priests held a consultation with the elders and scribes and the whole council. They bound Jesus, led him away, and handed him over to Pilate. [2] Pilate asked him, "Are you the King of the Jews?" He answered him, "You say so." [3] Then the chief priests accused him of many things. [4] Pilate asked him again, "Have you no answer? See how many charges they bring against you." [5] But Jesus made no further reply, so that Pilate was amazed.

[6] Now at the festival he used to release a prisoner for them, anyone for whom they asked. [7] Now a man called Barabbas was in prison with the rebels who had committed murder during the insurrection. [8] So the crowd came and began to ask Pilate to do for them according to his custom. [9] Then he answered them, "Do you want me to release for you the King of the Jews?" [10] For he realized that it was out of jealousy that the chief priests had handed him over. [11] But the chief priests stirred up the crowd to have him release Barabbas for them instead. [12] Pilate spoke to them again, "Then what do you wish me to do with the man you call the King of the Jews?" [13] They shouted back, "Crucify him!" [14] Pilate asked them, "Why, what evil has he done?" But they shouted all the more, "Crucify him!" [15] So Pilate, wishing to satisfy the crowd, released Barabbas for them; and after flogging Jesus, he handed him over to be crucified.

My God, My God!

[16] Then the soldiers led him into the courtyard of the palace (that is, the governor's headquarters); and they called together the whole cohort. [17] And they clothed him in a purple cloak; and after twisting some thorns into a crown, they put it on him. [18] And they began saluting him, "Hail, King of the Jews!" [19] They struck his head with a reed, spat upon him, and knelt down in homage to him. [20] After mocking him, they stripped him of the

purple cloak and put his own clothes on him. Then they led him out to crucify him.

²¹ They compelled a passer-by, who was coming in from the country, to carry his cross; it was Simon of Cyrene, the father of Alexander and Rufus. ²² Then they brought Jesus to the place called Golgotha (which means the place of a skull). ²³ And they offered him wine mixed with myrrh; but he did not take it. ²⁴ And they crucified him, and divided his clothes among them, casting lots to decide what each should take.

²⁵ It was nine o'clock in the morning when they crucified him. ²⁶ The inscription of the charge against him read, "The King of the Jews." ²⁷ And with him they crucified two bandits, one on his right and one on his left. ²⁹ Those who passed by derided him, shaking their heads and saying, "Aha! You who would destroy the temple and build it in three days, ³⁰ save yourself, and come down from the cross!" ³¹ In the same way the chief priests, along with the scribes, were also mocking him among themselves and saying, "He saved others; he cannot save himself. ³² Let the Messiah, the King of Israel, come down from the cross now, so that we may see and believe." Those who were crucified with him also taunted him.

³³ When it was noon, darkness came over the whole land until three in the afternoon. ³⁴ At three o'clock Jesus cried out with a loud voice, "Eloi, Eloi, lema sabachthani?" which means, "My God, my God, why have you forsaken me?" ³⁵ When some of the bystanders heard it, they said, "Listen, he is calling for Elijah." ³⁶ And someone ran, filled a sponge with sour wine, put it on a stick, and gave it to him to drink, saying, "Wait, let us see whether Elijah will come to take him down." ³⁷ Then Jesus gave a loud cry and breathed his last. ³⁸ And the curtain of the temple was torn in two, from top to bottom. ³⁹ Now when the centurion, who stood facing him, saw that in this way he breathed his last, he said, "Truly this man was God's Son!"

⁴⁰ There were also women looking on from a distance; among them were Mary Magdalene, and Mary the mother of James the younger and of Joses, and Salome. ⁴¹ These used to follow him and provided for him when he was in Galilee; and there were many other women who had come up with him to Jerusalem.

Questions for a Closer Look

1 Does Pilate really think that Jesus is a threat to the Roman government?

2 Is Pilate a strong person?

3 What might be the symbolism of the roles played by Barabbas and Simon of Cyrene?

4 Why is it only Jesus' death, rather than any of his miracles, that finally leads someone to recognize him as God's Son?

A Guide to the Reading

After agreeing that Jesus must die, the Jewish leaders take him to the Roman governor Pontius Pilate, who exercises supreme judicial authority in the region. They disagree with Jesus about religious matters, and Pilate would not care about such things, but they make an accusation that is sure to get his attention. They charge Jesus with claiming to be the king of the Jews (see 15:2).

Pilate interprets the title *king* to mean that Jesus wishes to overthrow the Roman occupation and set up a Jewish kingdom. Jesus does see himself as king, but he intends to establish his reign not on a battlefield but on a cross. So he does not really answer Pilate's question (15:2).

Once the term king is introduced, it rains down mercilessly on Jesus. Pilate sarcastically refers to him as "the King of the Jews" and puts that title above Jesus' head as the reason for his execution (15:12,26). The soldiers entertain themselves by dressing Jesus up as a king and bowing to him (15:16–19). As Jesus hangs gasping on the cross, some of the priests, presumably within earshot, say to each other, "Let the Messiah, the King of Israel, come down from the cross now, so that we may see and believe" (15:32). Those who make fun of Jesus and call him king are blind to his real kingship. They are blind to the fact that their making fun of him as king contributes to the coming of his kingdom.

The mysterious transaction at the cross is symbolized by the darkness that fills the sky (15:33). The darkness is a sign that judgment is taking place. God is bringing judgment on human hard-heartedness and sin, but the judgment is suffered by Jesus rather than by sinners. Jesus said that he would give his life as a ransom (10:45). On the cross he endures the judgment that falls on those who reject God, so that we might go free. Jesus suffers God's judgment of sin (14:36) so that we, who would otherwise have had to suffer it, may instead experience God's merciful and caring rule and live with God in a new bond of love. On the cross, Jesus drinks the cup of judgment so that we might drink the cup of salvation (10:38–39,45; 14:23–25).

Suffering pain of judgment, Jesus cries out the first line of Psalm 22: "My God, my God, why have you forsaken me?" (15:34). As far as any human eyes can see, including his own, God has abandoned him. Jesus has not sinned, but he experiences the separation from God that results from sin. The crowd's mockery adds humiliation to his physical pain.

The psalm that Jesus begins to pray goes on to declare confidence in God the savior (Psalm 22:22–31). Jesus feels abandoned by God, yet his praying Psalm 22 suggests that he continues to trust God, to cling to him as "my God."

Jesus dies for the disciples who have abandoned him, for the crowds who have rejected him, for the Romans who are executing him, even for the priests who stroll past his cross, mocking his kingship. Even those who condemn Jesus to death may be forgiven; indeed, it is Jesus' death that makes God's forgiveness available. No sin we could ever commit is beyond the range of the forgiveness accomplished at the cross.

Jesus breathes his last. Then remarkably, the soldier in charge of the execution squad exclaims, "Truly this man was God's Son!" (15:39). It is the first time in the Gospel that any human recognizes and acknowledges that Jesus is God's Son. By his death, Jesus has given himself entirely to God's purposes, at the greatest possible cost to himself. Thus he has demonstrated his relationship with God more clearly than he could have in any other way. At the heart of Jesus' sonship is obedience to and trust in his Father. The obedience and trust manifest in Jesus' manner of death have enabled the soldier to step out of the human way of thinking and into God's way of thinking. Through witnessing Jesus' death, the soldier has received the grace to perceive who Jesus is. God wants to give that grace to every one of us.

Questions for Application

1 Can a person feel abandoned by God? What effect might such an experience have on that person?

2 When have you seen someone demonstrate patience, love, and trust in God in the midst of suffering? How were you affected by this person?

3 How might God use some difficulty or suffering in your life for some good purpose? What might this reading say to you about this question?

4 What picture of Jesus have you drawn from reading Mark? Do you think it might change your relationship with Jesus?

5 How have the life and death of Jesus affected you? How will they affect decisions you will have to face in the future?

Approach to Prayer

Listen as a member of the group reads Mark 15:16–20. As a group, pray alound, "We adore you, O Christ, and we praise you, because by your holy cross you have redeemed the world." Listen as someone reads Mark 15:21–24 and repeat the same prayer. Do the same with Mark 15:25–32 and Mark 15:33–39. Finish by praying this ancient prayer along with the group:

Soul of Christ, sanctify me.
Body of Christ, save me.
Blood of Christ, inebriate me.
Water from the side of Christ,
    wash me.
Passion of Christ, strengthen me.
O good Jesus, hear me;
Within your wounds hide me;
Let me not be separated from
    you;
From the evil enemy defend me;
In the hour of my death call me
And bid me come to you,
So that with your saints I may
    praise you
Forever and ever. Amen.

Saints in the Making

The Meaning of the Cross
By Gerald Darring

Christians see the cross as a symbol of redemption. After studying the Holocaust in some depth, however, I became aware of another perspective on the cross: for centuries the cross was used by Christians as a means of persecuting the Jews. In the fourth century, the Roman emperor Constantine, as he was preparing for battle, had a vision of a cross in the sky and the words "In this sign you will conquer" written below. Thousands of Jews were slaughtered in the Crusades, the military campaign to bring back Christianity to the Holy Land, which took their name from the cloth crosses the soldiers wore on their uniforms. During the Inquisition in 15th-century Spain, Jews who refused to profess their belief in the cross were tortured and killed. My awareness of these misuses of the cross made it difficult for me to maintain my reverence for it until I happened to come upon the story of a Christian woman who risked her life during the Holocaust.

Maria Maciarz was a Polish woman living in Warsaw during World War II. Her daughter-in-law had agreed to hide a Jewish boy in her apartment after the boy's parents decided to flee Poland to escape the Nazis. The daughter-in-law became scared that if she was caught with the Jewish child in her home, she would be put to death, so she decided to turn the boy in to the Gestapo, the Nazi secret police. Maria stopped her, however, and took the boy into her own apartment, where she hid him until the end of the war. The boy's parents miraculously survived the Holocaust and came looking for him after the war. They found him being lovingly cared for by Maria. The couple planned to leave Poland to start a new life elsewhere, and they signed their family house over to Maria as a token of gratitude for saving their son's life. When it came time for Maria to sign the deed, she signed by drawing a cross; she could neither read nor write.

Over the centuries, the cross has often been misinterpreted as a sign of victory over others and a symbol of Christian superiority. Nothing could be further from the true message of the cross of Jesus Christ. Maria may not have been able to read or write, but she had something many others did not: a profound understanding of the true meaning of the cross. In *that* sign, I could believe.

A Surprise Ending

Mark Leaves Us with Questions

At his last meal, Jesus gave his followers an insight into the meaning of the death that awaited him. He was going to his death in obedience to God. With gesture and interpretation, Jesus showed that his death would create a new relationship between God and human beings: "He took a cup, and after giving thanks he gave it to them, and all of them drank from it. He said to them, 'This is my blood of the covenant, which is poured out for many'" (14:23–24). Jesus showed that he expected his death to bring God's Kingdom, for he implied that he would eat his next meal with his followers in the kingdom: "Truly I tell you, I will never again drink of the fruit of the vine until that day when I drink it new in the kingdom of God" (14:25).

Mark assures us in his brief conclusion that these expectations have begun to be fulfilled. Jesus has completed his surprising announcement of God's Kingdom with another huge surprise: after dying, he has risen from the dead. Through his death and resurrection, he has accomplished all that he promised.

While Jesus' resurrection is *the* great surprise at the end of Mark's Gospel, the ending is surprising in other respects also. In order to see this, it is necessary to recognize that Mark's Gospel has two endings: the ending that Mark himself wrote, 16:1–8, and a longer ending, 16:9–20, which seems to have been added by an early editor of the Gospel. The Church recognizes the longer ending as inspired Scripture; it belongs to the canon of the New Testament as much as the rest of Mark's Gospel does. But to grasp the message that Mark himself wished to communicate, we should pay close attention to the way he brought his account to a close. Mark's own ending, which seems abrupt, has something to teach us.

16:1 When the sabbath was over, Mary Magdalene, and Mary the mother of James, and Salome bought spices, so that they might go and anoint him. 2 And very early on the first day of the week, when the sun had risen, they went to the tomb. [3] They had been saying to one another, "Who will roll away the stone for us from the entrance to the tomb?" [4] When they looked up, they saw that the stone, which was very large, had already been rolled back. [5] As they entered the tomb, they saw a young man, dressed in a white robe, sitting on the right side; and they were alarmed. [6] But he said to them, "Do not be alarmed; you are looking for Jesus of Nazareth, who was crucified. He has been raised; he is not here. Look, there is the place they laid him. [7] But go, tell his disciples and Peter that he is going ahead of you to Galilee; there you will see him, just as he told you." [8] So they went out and fled from the tomb, for terror and amazement had seized them; and they said nothing to anyone, for they were afraid.

Two remarkable features of this account are the presence of the women and the absence of Jesus.

The women had stood at a distance from Jesus' cross (15:40). Some scholars argue that these women may have been with Jesus and the male disciples at the Last Supper. Mark does not mention women at the meal, but it was normal for women to share the Passover meal with men, so we cannot conclude anything from Mark's silence on the matter. We do know that many women had accompanied Jesus to Jerusalem for the festival (15:41), and there would have been room for at least some of them at the meal, for Jesus had arranged for a large room (14:15). In any case, a few women had watched him die and had also witnessed his burial (15:47).

In Mark's conclusion the women come to the tomb two days after Jesus' death, intending to honor him by placing aromatic spices in the wrappings around his body (16:1). While these women have shown more loyalty to Jesus than his male followers, they seem utterly unprepared for what they discover at the tomb (16:5). The announcement of Jesus' resurrection breaks upon them as a terrifying revelation (16:8). Now it is their turn to run away (16:8; compare 14:50).

Evidently the women do eventually report on what they found at the tomb (as the later editor confirms in 16:10). And when they do, the fact that they were not expecting Jesus to rise from the dead will make their testimony believable. The angel was hardly a figment of hopeful imaginations.

Indeed, the women's very presence in Mark's account is a strong indicator of its factual basis. At that time, women were not considered competent to offer legal testimony. Thus, if anyone were to try to lend credibility to fiction, he would hardly invent a group of female witnesses.

As to Mark's "failure" to provide an account of the risen Jesus, it may not have seemed as strange to his first readers as it does to us. Scholars think it quite possible that Mark's was the first Gospel to be written. In this case, his readers did not have the other three Gospels with which to compare it. Unlike us, Mark's first readers would not expect that a Gospel *should* end with a description of Jesus after his resurrection.

We must conclude that Mark viewed his brief account of the empty tomb as sufficient to serve his purposes. He wished to show that Jesus' death achieved its goal. The empty tomb and the angel's announcement that Jesus has risen from the dead confirmed that Jesus achieved his objective. Jesus now lives as God's Son in the glory of his kingdom. The reconciliation with God that lies at the heart of God's Kingdom is available to all. God's reign over men and women, which Jesus proclaimed to be near, has now arrived.

This is not to say that Mark thought God's Kingdom had ceased to be a somewhat hidden, even paradoxical, reality. As it was during Jesus' earthly life, God's reign is now-but-not-yet-completely-now. The complete coming of the kingdom lies ahead of us at Jesus' return (8:38). But from the moment of his resurrection, Jesus begins to gather his followers into a community of trust and obedience to God and of humble service to others. United to him, this community is now the new temple, filled with God's presence and praise. Exercising his ongoing leadership over this community, Jesus will meet his disciples in Galilee (16:7), that is, in the ordinary circumstances of their lives. He will continue to lead this community in all the Galilees of the world.

Mark, it seems, wrote his Gospel with two ideas in mind: to help us be confident that the risen Jesus is now leading us on a mission for God's Kingdom, and to help us accept the cross as the starting point for that mission, which looks toward a kingdom not yet fully arrived.

While the absence of a description of the risen Jesus may at first strike us as a shortcoming in Mark's conclusion, in its own way it carries a distinct message. A picture of the risen Jesus might tend to displace in our minds the picture that Mark has already given us. With his empty-tomb ending, Mark leaves us thinking of Jesus with his disciples as they visited the villages of Galilee, walked the roads, and spent their final days in Jerusalem. Mark has given us these scenes of Jesus with his followers in the various settings of their ordinary lives in order to convey his final message: the risen Jesus is with us in the ordinary settings of *our* lives.

Unfinished Business

Jesus and His Followers at the End of Mark's Gospel

The ending that Mark himself gave to his Gospel leaves the story of Jesus' relationship with his disciples unresolved. When Jesus is arrested, his male disciples run away (14:50). The last we see of any of them in Mark's Gospel is Peter, weeping after denying that he knows Jesus (14:72). At least a few of the women disciples remain with Jesus as he dies, watching from a distance (15:40–41). But at the very end the women run away too and do not deliver the report that the angel charges them with (16:8). Mark ends with the startling statement that "they told nothing to anyone, for they were frightened."

This sudden ending, which leaves important threads dangling, spurs us to ask, "Then what?"

Like us, Mark's original readers probably already knew part of the answer. Eventually the women must have gotten over their fright and told the male disciples what had happened at the tomb; for how else could the incident have become known? Then too, the angel spoke about a meeting between the risen Jesus and his followers that would take place in Galilee (16:7). Mark's readers, being Christians, would have heard about such appearances of Jesus after his resurrection. It is even possible that Mark's original readers heard about these appearances from Peter himself. If the tradition that Mark wrote in Rome is correct, Mark's first readers would have been Roman Christians, who might have had a chance to hear Peter's testimony when he was in Rome before his martyrdom there.

Still, Mark leaves us guessing about what happened when Jesus met his followers in Galilee.

The angel's words in 16:7 ("Go, tell his disciples and Peter that he is going ahead of you to Galilee; there you will see him, just as he told you") suggest that Jesus reconciles the disciples to himself. They had abandoned him before the crucifixion, but now, after the Resurrection, Jesus will put that past behind them and they will move on in their relationship.

The disciples seem to finally understand who Jesus is. They had recognized Jesus as Messiah but had not expected a suffering messiah. They had not known Jesus as the Son of God who would show his utter trust in and obedience to his Father by laying down his life. Seeing the crucified-but-risen one in Galilee, they would be able for the first time to grasp who he really is. They may also, at the same time, have gained an understanding of themselves and what it means to be a disciple of Jesus.

In Galilee, we may suppose, the risen Jesus gave his disciples a new chance. He forgave them, healed their spiritual sight, and restored their relationship with him.

There is a circularity to the Gospel of Mark. What occurs at the beginning occurs again after the end. Jesus' first act, after announcing that the kingdom was near, was to call disciples (1:16–20). His first act after rising from the dead will be to gather his disciples around him again. The Gospel begins with John's call to repentance, soon followed by Jesus' acts of forgiveness. The Gospel ends with Jesus' followers, who need to repent, receiving the promise of a meeting with Jesus (16:7) at which they can be reconciled with him.

Perhaps Mark constructed his Gospel in this somewhat circular way because he thought there is also a circularity to the Christian life. His first readers already knew that Jesus is the Messiah and Son of God. They were already committed to following him. But it is possible to make an initial commitment to follow Jesus without understanding thoroughly what that means—or recognizing how unprepared one is to do it. Following Jesus involves a process of discovering that he is somewhat different from what we expect, a process of stumbling along the way, receiving his help and forgiveness, and coming to a deeper knowledge of him. Mark wrote to help his readers reflect on this process. His Gospel was a tool for examining their successes and failures in following Jesus and coming to deeper conversion.

As Mark shows, Jesus' first disciples did not get it the first time around. Presumably they did not get it all the second time either. Nor did Mark's first readers, who lived a generation or so later. Nor do we, 20 centuries later.

Like Jesus' first disciples and Mark's first readers, we experience Jesus' call. We set out to follow Jesus, but we inevitably run into difficulties. The kingdom that he leads us into, while filled with God's power, is hidden. God's power sometimes removes evil, but the kingdom often manifests itself by enabling us to respond to evil with love, patience, courage, and forgiveness. The kingdom continues to come, as it did through Jesus, through suffering and death. Grasping this kingdom requires faith. It requires seeing things as God sees them, not as we are inclined to see them. Cooperating with Jesus in the coming of this kingdom involves denying ourselves and living for a fulfillment that is yet to come. It involves obedience to God, trust in God, humble service to other people, and participation in a community of fellow followers, the Church.

Talking about all this may be easy. But as soon as we give it a try, we find out how difficult it is. Our blindness to God's ways of working is exposed. Our tendency to look out for ourselves first, our desire to be in charge, our avoidance of grimy, thankless tasks, our thirst for recognition, our fear of identifying ourselves with an unpopular position, our cowardice—all these ordinary, human tendencies immediately come to the surface. It turns out to be much easier to acknowledge Jesus in church on Sunday morning than to seize the weekday opportunities to trust him and serve other people. In real life, the way the suffering Son of God wishes to work is often not very obvious to us or, if we notice it, not very appealing.

So we fail, as Jesus' first disciples did. Like Peter, we may sometimes feel bitterly disappointed with ourselves. We discover our need for conversion. Having experienced our blindness and hard-heartedness, we turn back to Jesus for forgiveness and healing. We too go through a cycle of repentance and reconciliation with him.

This process is what Jesus is about in our lives, as he was in the lives of his first disciples. He foresees our failures as clearly as he foresaw those of his first followers. He is still as Mark shows him: a patient teacher, always willing to forgive, realistic about his followers' shortcomings and hidden flaws but never harsh.

Saint Thérèse of Lisieux writes, "This daring ambition of aspiring to great sanctity has never left me. I do not rely on my own merits, because I haven't any. I put all my confidence in him who is virtue, who is holiness itself. My feeble efforts are all he wants; he can lift me up to his side and, by clothing me with his own boundless merits, make a saint of me."

Mark's message, his good news, is that Jesus died as a ransom to establish a bond between God and us. When we stumble in our efforts to follow him, we become especially conscious that this ransom is just what we need. So we can be glad that Jesus ate the Passover with his followers and gave himself to them wholly—and continues to give himself to us in the Eucharist. We can be glad that Jesus met his disciples in Galilee after their failure and reconciled them to himself—and continues to meet us in the Sacrament of Reconciliation. After his resurrection, Jesus went ahead of the disciples to Galilee, the ordinary sphere of their lives, to lead them on a mission with him. We can be glad that he meets us today wherever we live and keeps calling us to follow him.

Listening When God Speaks

As you have worked your way through this book, you have been listening to God's word. But this is not the first time that God has spoken to you, and indeed God has been speaking to you throughout your young life. Let's look at some of the ways in which God speaks to you, and let's look at some of the ways in which you can improve your listening skills

The most obvious way in which you receive messages from God is through the Scripture, which is the Word of God. The people of Israel and the early Christians recorded their experiences of God's saving acts in history, and our religious tradition accepts their writings as God's Word to us. We believe that when we read Scripture, or hear it read, God is communicating his Word to us. It would be a good thing for you to develop the habit of reading the Bible on a regular basis, and you should make every effort to benefit from the weekly reading of Scripture at Mass.

An excellent way in which to listen to God speaking to us in Scripture is to pray the Scripture. Begin by adopting a proper prayer *posture* through the selection of an appropriate time and place for prayer. Once in the proper posture, become aware of God's *presence* in your life and in the time and place you have chosen for your prayer. Then *pray* for guidance from the Holy Spirit, asking help to understand the passage on which you will be reading and reflecting. You are now ready to read your selected *passage*, but you must read slowly and deliberately, with the intention of hearing God's voice in the passage. After you have read and reread the passage, *pause* for reflection on the passage. Allow time for God to speak to you through the words of the text.

The Bible is the Word of God, but it is not the only Word of God. Jesus Christ is also the Word of God, the Word made flesh. The Gospel of John begins with that message: "In the beginning was the Word, and the Word was with God, and the Word was

God. . . . And the Word became flesh and made his dwelling among us." We want, then, to listen to God speaking to us in Jesus Christ and one good way to do that is by participating fully in Mass. Gathering together with the other worshipers, we enter into communion with them and with the presiding priest. The words and actions of the celebration put our spirits at rest, so that by the time we enter into communion with Christ in the Eucharist, we are in a position to hear God's message of love, peace, and salvation. We should not make the mistake of thinking that Jesus speaks to us only at the moment of receiving the Eucharist. His voice can be heard—if only we listen—through the community, through the priest, through the entire Eucharistic celebration, and finally, bringing it all together, in the eating and drinking of the Body and Blood of Christ.

Because the Church is the Body of Christ, we can also speak of the Church as the Word of God. God speaks to us through the community of believers, and in a special way through the leadership of that community. One way to listen to the voice of God in the Church is by paying attention to the voices of the believers nearest us: our parents and teachers, our parish priest, and the people we worship with on Sunday. Another way is to stay in touch with what the leadership of our Church is teaching. The bishops of our Church, especially the Bishop of Rome, the Holy Father, and our own local bishop, the leader of the Church where we are active, speak to us in words that have the authority of the Word of God; as Catholics we hear in them the voice of God.

Finally, God speaks to us in our own life experiences. The Second Vatican Council recovered the biblical image of "reading the signs of the times," that is, hearing the voice of God in the events of history. On the personal level, we can hear God speaking to us in such things as our encounters with others, our decisions, our successes and failures, and the challenges arising from the difficulties of life. To hear God's voice in our life experiences, we need to pay attention to those experiences, reflect on them, and learn from them.

There is a wonderful story in the Old Testament about a young boy named Samuel. (You can read it in 1 Samuel 3.) Samuel was assisting an old priest named Eli, who was waiting in the Temple for God to speak to him. One night while he was sleeping, Samuel heard someone call him. He assumed it was Eli, so he went and woke Eli up to find out what he wanted. Eli responded that he had not called, and he sent the boy back to bed. After a while Samuel heard his name called again, but once more Eli told the boy that it was not him. When it happened a third time, Eli knew that it was God calling to Samuel, and he said to the boy, "Go to sleep, and if you are called, reply, 'Speak, LORD, for your servant is listening.'"

The first thing to notice about this story is that everybody expected God to speak to the old priest, but God spoke to the young boy instead. It is important that you be receptive in your youth to the voice of God and not think that God will only speak to you "later." God is speaking to you now—in the Scriptures, in Jesus Christ, in the Church, and in your life experiences.

The other point of the story is that, in order to hear God speaking to us, we must be listening. Samuel would never have received God's message if he had not listened, and the same thing applies to us. Our lives are busy, with plenty of noise. We need to learn how to cut through all the noise and listen to God speaking to us.

Resources

Bibles

The following editions of the Bible contain the full set of biblical books recognized by the Catholic Church, along with a great deal of useful explanatory material:

- The Catholic Youth Bible (Saint Mary's Press), which can be ordered with either the New American Bible or the New Revised Standard Version

- Student Bible for Catholics (Thomas Nelson Publishers), which uses the text of the New American Bible

- The Catholic Study Bible (Oxford University Press), which uses the text of the New American Bible

- The Catholic Bible: Personal Study Edition (Oxford University Press), which also uses the text of the New American Bible

Additional Sources

- Mueller, Steve. "Exploring the Synoptic Gospels: Mark and His Careful Readers," *Scripture from Scratch* (Cincinnati, Ohio: St. Anthony Messenger Press, January 2000).

- Singer-Towns, Brian. "Mark's Gospel: First and Fast," *Youth Update* (Cincinnati, Ohio: St. Anthony Messenger Press, December 2002).

- Van Linden, Phililp A., C.M. *Gospel According to Mark* (Collegeville, Minn.: Liturgical Press, 1985).

Available in the Six Weeks with the Bible for Catholic Teens series

Theme: God Reveals Himself to Us

Genesis 1–11: God Makes a Start
ISBN-13: 978-0-8294-2050-0; ISBN-10: 0-8294-2050-9

Exodus: God to the Rescue
ISBN-13: 978-0-8294-2051-7; ISBN-10: 0-8294-2051-7

Luke: The Good News of God's Mercy
ISBN-13: 978-0-8294-2052-4; ISBN-10: 0-8294-2052-5

Revelation: God's Gift of Hope
ISBN-13: 978-0-8294-2049-4; ISBN-10: 0-8294-2049-5

Theme: Jesus and His Disciples

Mark: Getting to Know Jesus
ISBN-13: 978-0-8294-2082-1; ISBN-10: 0-8294-2082-7

John 1–10: I Am the Bread of Life
ISBN-13: 978-0-8294-2083-8; ISBN-10: 0-8294-2083-5

John 11–21: My Peace I Give You
ISBN-13: 978-0-8294-2084-5; ISBN-10: 0-8294-2084-3

Acts: The Good News of the Holy Spirit
ISBN-13: 978-0-8294-2085-2; ISBN-10: 0-8294-2085-1

For more information or to order, please call 800-621-1008. Volume discounts available.